Inspired by Antiques

Inspired by Antiques

confidently combining the old and the new

Caroline Clifton-Mogg

photography by Fritz von der Schulenburg

RYLAND
PETERS
& SMALL

Publishing Director **Anne Ryland**
Senior Designer **Larraine Shamwana**
Senior Editor **Sian Parkhouse**
Location Researchers **Nadine Bazar**
and **Kate Brunt**
Production **Rosanna Dickinson**
Illustrator **Caroline McAdam Clark**

First published in Great Britain
in 1999 by
Ryland Peters & Small, Cavendish
House, 51–55 Mortimer Street,
London W1N 7TD

ISBN 1 84172 001 1

A catalogue record for this book is
available from the British Library.

Printed in China. Produced by Sun Fung
Offset Binding Co. Ltd.

Jacket Photography
Front and back: Frédéric Méchiche's homes in
Paris and near Toulon; *front flap inset*: John
Rosselli's house in New Jersey.

Contents

Introduction

Rooms have always been self portraits – ever since St Jerome walked into his study, hung up his hat and sat down at his desk while his lion looked sleepily on, there has never been a room anywhere in the world that did not have something to say about its owner. Sometimes the portrait is pleasurable, sometimes less so, but most of us, whether knowingly or not, will strive to ensure that the picture we paint in our own homes will be satisfying – to ourselves at the very least, if not to anybody else.

decorated. But so popular is it now, and so widely is the information disseminated, that all too often it seems that the more we read and the more we hear, the more confused we become. Interior decoration today sometimes feels like one of those multiple-choice quizzes where every question has three or four possible answers. With so many different possibilities no wonder it sometimes seems easier to simply go for the safest option, no matter how visually unsatisfying that may be.

American antique dealer John Rosselli understands completely the art of arranging (below left and right). Set off by the languorous beauty of his dogs (who look as if they are posing for a Sargent portrait) is a vastly mixed group of objects and furniture that works perfectly.

English antique dealer Christopher Gibbs is renowned for his taste: in the hall of his Oxfordshire house is a group of old and new, East and West, that appears immediately welcoming (right).

No corner is too small to make interesting in Piero Castellini Baldissera's Tuscan house (far right top and centre). Small objects might be lost on their own, but together they make an appealing picture.

Which is where interior decoration enters the argument. Since the late 19th century (which was around the time interested people with a certain talent and flair, both in Europe and America, started writing books and advising others on how their houses should look), the art or science of interior decoration has become more and more absorbing to all those of us who have a space – any sort of space – that can be

During the 17th and 18th centuries taste was prescribed by architects and upholsterers, who dictated each detail of an entire scheme. Today, our view is more eclectic, but such eclecticism can bring confusion to even the most assured, and raise such knotty questions as: What goes with what? What can be used together? Should new and old be displayed separately? Should the new and cheap be resigned to being simply the utilitarian, the useful, whilst anything valuable or old is displayed as an icon and preserved like a fly in amber. And what about different cultures? Surely it is not possible to live with things so dissimilar as an oversized old Chinese oil jar, and a 19th-century European wooden country chair in the same room? And how do we know?

By definition of its longevity, anything old – even something as little as thirty or forty years old – has an individuality and a presence. We are defined by the past, not the present – although as leading British decorator Robert Kime says, the past can be a minute ago. Equally, furniture or objects from another place or country – made by someone of whom we know nothing – have a romance and a history not shared by our own familiar High Street possessions. The acquisitive nature of anyone interested in design and decoration knows that living with all these different things around us gives a pleasure and satisfaction that cannot be found when surrounded only with the ubiquitous results of modern mass production.

In decorator Annie Kuentzman-Levet's Normandy house (above), unusual objects are grouped in an harmonious white group which is accented by the single rose toile de Jouy curtain.

The things that we see around us should be looked at not just in their functional role, but also as objects in their own decorative right. Antique dealer and decorator Christopher Hodsoll uses the wrought-iron curve of his 19th-century staircase in London to frame a piece of Victorian engineering brilliance (top).

The most ordinary and most eclectic of objects are formed into irresistible combinations of simple pleasure (above and above right).

Everyone knows someone whose taste seems to be so much better than one's own. These lucky people seem to have the knack of just grouping the most disparate objects, lights and furniture – things that look as though they would not go together in a hundred years – and of making them look absolutely wonderful, as if they had always been meant to be in the place they find themselves. It is possible, of course, that some of these lucky few have natural taste – just as some people are natural painters or cooks – but it does not mean that others cannot learn. Hence

this book. It is the case that almost anyone can acquire good taste, both by instruction and by observation, and in *Inspired by Antiques* we – or rather those with the knack – demonstrate how they combine things from different times and places into a look that is absolutely of today. For this book we have taken all completely new photographs in the houses of some of the most influential interior decorators, architects and designers working in Britain, France, Italy and the USA, recording and noting their unique ways of doing things.

Each of our subjects has his or her individual style, but what is common to them all is that none of them is bound by conventional rules of fashion or association. They will all place, with seeming haphazardness, a valuable antique next to something new; a piece of junk against a

Combining textures is important: John Rosselli mixes the weight of iron with blue-and-white ceramic urns and greenery, all back-lit from the daylight outside (below).

The simple beauty of these early American salt glazed pots next to an iron figure originally used to roast small birds needs no other embellishment (bottom).

There can be a beauty in the grouping of even the most utilitarian of objects. Annie Kuentzman-Levet, in her Normandy garden, combines antique glass cloches with hand-thrown terracotta flower pots (below right).

treasure, an Eastern artefact with a piece of uncompromisingly Western origin. And in their hands, it works, for good interior decorators, antique dealers, and those lucky people with innate confidence have always known that there is no rule which says you must decorate in only one style or period, or not dare to mix the unmixable. You can – it is modern, it is what contemporary style and taste is all about. And what this book is about too.

Whether it is a large Welsh oak dresser, a small china jug, or a brightly coloured Mexican rug most people, in one way or another, own something which is either old or from another place. Perhaps it is an heirloom, or a present or

even something bought on irresistible impulse somewhere in the world, and it may be worth quite a lot, or practically nothing at all. One person's junk is another's treasures after all. But whatever it is and however acquired, if it comes from somewhere else, it has a past, and, as such, is part of the fabric of our present lives.

Decorating in this way is decorating with life. There is room for everything, and learning how to use all these objects – new, old, antiques and souvenirs – is about intimacy; an intimacy that comes from combining different times and places together. Therein lies the inspiration; this is the charm and the magic, and this is what decorating with antiques is about.

Arranging
Antiques

The idea of anyone even thinking about how to arrange – never mind re-arrange - the furniture in a room, is in itself a relatively new concept. Up until the 17th century, only the rich and noble had furniture to speak of; ordinary people had few pieces, and these were strictly utilitarian, and many fulfilled several purposes simultaneously. A chest, for example, could be somewhere to store linen, a bench to sit on, and sometimes even a bed. But gradually interior decoration and the design of all parts of a room, from the walls to the furniture, become more important (mark the fabled rooms of Louis XIV's Versailles) and by the 18th century architects and master cabinetmakers, many of whom worked very closely together, were designing furniture that was every bit as influential in the context of a room as the walls and ceiling. Furniture was now considered an integral part of the decoration of the room, whether the grand reception rooms of Robert Adam (1728–92) or the small, intimate, almost secret cabinets to be found in larger French, Italian or German houses.

Indeed, at this time – the golden period of Robert Adam and William Kent (1685–1748) – many pieces of furniture, usually designed and made on commission for a particular client and house, were intended solely for a particular position in a room, a position from which they were rarely to

In the 18th-century flat of a Parisian collector with a most confident eye (opposite), the most unusual things – a 1950's Sèvres vase, furniture designed by Carlo Bugatti and the steely head of a unicorn – all go together with panache.

East and West share the same aesthetic: in this London flat (above), the gauzy four-poster is guarded by Eastern chests and flanked by Chinese pots that act as tables.

A fine piece can stand alone without additional back-up, like this chair against a background of books in decorator Bunny William's Connecticut barn (centre left).

Hand-painted canvas walls in this Long Island cottage are the background for a fairytale gothic bed with its 19th-century headboard (below left).

Artist Frank Faulkner uses weight and height to build up different, and disparate, objects and furniture into a group of pleasing proportions (right).

be moved. Indeed some pieces remained in one place for the whole of their or their owners' lives. There was no thought of having a useful little piece that might suit one purpose for a few years, and then another later on.

By the mid-19th century this decorative discipline had given way to an apparent urge to put as much furniture, in as many different styles as possible, into one room. It looked, frankly, a mess; and perhaps inevitably, there was a reaction against such confused taste, with such pundits as Augustus Welby Pugin (1812–52) and William Morris (1834–96) calling for a new simplicity and a return to the aesthetic values of the past. In our own century, we also have seen many decorative contrasts, veering from rooms with so little furniture as to be almost sparse to the giddy heights or depths of the so-called

'country house look' where, at its nadir, there might be in a room almost as many small chairs, tables and swagged and draped knick-knacks as would have been found in 1870.

But it seems there is once again a new mood in interior decoration: our prosperous society gives us a plethora of both information and choice, the net result being there is no longer any one right way to arrange furniture, nor any one 'right' way to put things together. Instead, it is just as you yourself want to see it. The small, the large, the new, the old, the sophisticated, the ethnic; all can be used together, if you know how. Those with confidence mix with brio. There are, of course, degrees of mixing – some mix pieces that are nearly alike in type, period or style, and some combine things which are completely opposing and in strong contrast: like

French decorator Frédéric Méchiche understands how to mix pieces from different periods and cultures in a way that is both interesting, unusual and, above all, comfortable (far left and left). In his Paris apartment, sanded and waxed wooden floors and plain white painted panelled walls form a restful backdrop to furniture and objects ranging from the 1st century to the 1960s.

In a monochromatic group, the 18th century in the form of the panelling and the grey marble fireplace meets the 20th, represented by a Sèvres vase designed in the 1950s and metalwork-framed chairs and firedogs designed in the 1940s (above).

the 18th and 20th centuries. Some will put together lines that flow with severe angularity, and some prefer the juxtaposition of different continents – African and Europe.

Nothing is without use or charm. While this is not a book about using junk, it is instructive to note how good designers appreciate everything for what it is: Christopher Gibbs keeps horses' leather lawn shoes on a window sill in his hall; Christopher Hodsoll lines up shells and blowfish on his dining room sideboard. These things are not necessarily of great value, but they are of interest both in shape and design – and in the way that they are shown. William Morris famously said 'Have nothing in your houses that you do not know to be useful, or believe to be beautiful', but he might also have added that you should also only have things which you really like, for then you will always be able to find how to best use them.

Furniture

Glass and wood, metal and gilt – all come together in a Normandy living room (above).

Any colour as long as it's white (right). A chaise longue, two apothecary's chests used one on top of each other and assorted white vases and jugs, accented by touches of steely blue, come together in a remarkably calm and harmonious manner.

It is one of the perversities of life that when surrounded by the new and accessible, we are drawn toward the old and the unusual. So we should and can use different pieces of furniture and furnishings in the way which suits us most – mixing styles, periods and textures – until we arrive at a look that is right for our own individual lives. Pieces from different times and cultures can work together. It is all a question of scale and harmony.

tables

Tables – whether splendid long boards used for leisurely meals or little three-legged pieces of furniture that looked more like stools – first appeared in classical Greece in the 4th century AD. They were highly prized items and the finest materials were used for their tops – porphyry, wood or marble. The Ancient Romans' tables were even more splendid, with carved legs in the form of feet and claws, ornamented with gold, silver and bronze. Renaissance designers in Italy and France, inspired by these classical designs, embellished them still further with more gold and precious stones.

Later, in England, medieval tables were of the most basic construction. Used only for the purposes of eating, they were usually made in the form of a portable trestle. In even the most wealthy of palaces, when the table was laid for a grand dinner, beneath the damask cloth and the gold and silver plate might well have been a fairly rough board on trestles. Later this single table became more solid – an immoveable prop, standing on sturdy legs and used both for meals and also as a place at which to conduct business.

Refined society, however, demanded more variety in furniture and, by the 18th century, tables, like chairs, had become ubiquitous and were now being produced in different heights and shapes. New, more sophisticated methods of construction meant that tables could be more flexible; they were no longer bound to be heavy and static. The immoveable refectory table gave way to lighter-weight tables that could be set up in whichever room one might care to eat.

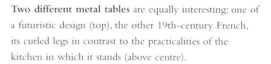

Two different metal tables are equally interesting: one of a futuristic design (top), the other 19th-century French, its curled legs in contrast to the practicalities of the kitchen in which it stands (above centre).

A simple English folding table is matched with a French 18th-century chair and Louis XVI lantern (left); while the tile-topped wooden table (above) is dressed with a zinc-framed mirror, *trompe-l'oeil* beribboned oval frames and other objects, all of which have a certain transparency.

The dining room in Frédéric Méchiche's Paris flat is a perfect example of flexible eating. Metal and glass tables, designed and made by Méchiche on a modular principle, can be moved around and regrouped according to need and the mood of the moment. One square table is used in a setting for three (above), and two tables used together make a more formal arrangement (left). The rectangular lines of the 18th-century painted panelling and the corresponding lines of the 18th-century painted chairs are at one with the minimalist design of the tables. Contemporary silver and glass tie the styles together.

Now there were also tables that could stand in the centre of the room where you could sew, read or play cards; tables that could be placed beside chairs from which tea and coffee could be served; and decorative tables to stand against walls, between windows or doors – for tables by now had two different guises. There were still those which were essentially practical, but now there were also those which were made purely as objects of beauty; not expected to be pressed into much service, but designed merely to stand, shine and be admired.

This is still the case, but perhaps in today's life and rooms there is, generally, less space for everything. A dining table, for example, is a major and pretty basic piece of furniture and no matter how expensive, it is in essence simply a long surface that dominates any room in which it stands. It will be used for meals, obviously, and

also perhaps for working at, but unless it is very fine or beautiful, it will probably look better, when not in use, to have something or things sitting on it which will distract the eye from one undiluted expanse of wood.

A lengthy rectangular table can often look better standing alongside a wall than floating loosely in the room. Against the wall, in place of a cabinet or desk, it becomes an important element of the room instead of an interloper, and it can then be used as a base from which to build up a scheme, using tall lamps, figures, objects, ceramics, pictures and flowers or plants. It is important to balance the mass of a table with an element of pattern on the wall behind it. It might be one large picture or a group of smaller ones, a wall hanging, a curtain or even a mirror. Whatever you choose, the size of the group should be in proportion with the table.

Another way to reconcile a long table in a busy room is to have one which stands behind a sofa – a very useful device this, as long as the table is long enough not to be dwarfed by the sofa, and not too narrow so as to be insignificant. It also must not be taller than the height of the sofa back. A table placed thus is particularly useful in a room where storage space is at a premium, as the space underneath can be utilized. Designer Christophe Gollut covers his dining table with a floor-length cloth, and he not only covers the entire surface with lamps, books and objects, but he also uses the now hidden space he has created below as an instant cupboard for storing all manner of living room essentials.

A round table that could be used for eating, working or reading was not widely popular in either France or England, the principal sources of influences on table design and construction,

A quirky piece of furniture like this rustic wooden twig table with a polished wooden top (far left), is seen all the more clearly when placed beside a simple but sophisticated day bed covered in sharp yellow on a ground of pale terracotta floor tiles in this Italian house.

An exercise in scale: a corner table is placed beside a half-size chair (left). On the table is a group of candlesticks of differing heights, which contribute height to the composition. The saffron coloured chair seat, defined by dark piping, matches the wall colour almost exactly.

John Rosselli knows well how to use the sophisticated with the simple to make a group of contrast and interest (above). In his summer barn he combines, against clapboard walls, and on a heavy oak console table, such diverse pieces as a large blue and white majolica urn converted into a light, two tole lilies in their pots – also blue and white – and ornamental figures. They are all firmly anchored by a wall mirror set in a heavy frame.

A circular dining table is rendered interesting in its own right by the addition of an ornamental birdcage used as a centrepiece, surrounded by books and other tactile objects (above right). Notice that the dining chairs are upholstered in different fabrics.

In a Mississippi plantation house decorated by Vicente Wolf, a fine 17th-century Spanish table with a bust of Marie Antoinette is dramatically framed and reflected by a full-length modern mirror, arranged to lean insouciantly against the wall (right).

until the beginning of the 19th century, when the benefits of having a light portable table that could be called into various service as and when circumstance demanded began to be realized. When used in a living room an 'occasional' table, as it came to be called, was often covered in piles of books – sometimes ranged in too regular a form to be pleasing to the eye. Today the table can be covered with any manner of things – interesting things, pretty things, unusual things – displayed on their own, or grouped on trays and plates that can easily be moved if the table is needed. Use it still as an extension to your library, but piles of books of different heights become immediately more accessible, more decorative, than regimented

blocks. Intersperse the piles with jugs of flowers, a terracotta figure or a small painting on an easel. Do this, and suddenly the boring table is part of the scheme of things – an integral element of the room.

What you put on a table depends on its shape and height. As with all aspects of interior decoration, proportion and harmony are the important things. Obviously on a small, fragile side table, a heavy lamp and a large bronze figure would look wrong; and on a heavy solid table, your prized collection of egg cups might not have the dramatic effect you intended. Although proportion is, of course, important, symmetry is less so. Tables that are placed either end of a sofa or beside armchairs need not match,

A small iron table forms the centrepiece of this updated neoclassical group (far left). The chairs, the lamp, the screen with its Greek key design, and even the design of the toile de Jouy, all work together.

In a London flat, a table of exactly bed height and night-table size (left) has been made from a tall Chinese pot. In the same way lights can be made from a range of jars and vases, so can a table be contrived from the unexpected and unusual.

An Eastern table has been made into a studied and formal arrangement by using a selection of Eastern shapes using baskets, pots and boxes, mixed with a distinctly Western lamp (below left).

A shiny metal modern take on an old-fashioned butler's tray is placed to good effect against a determinedly antique painted radiator and panelled figured wood walls and a wooden floor in a Manhattan apartment (below).

In a large room there may be many different tables and it is important that you do not forget to see them. Side tables in particular are often simply seen as practical adjuncts to living and are therefore often disregarded or perceived as things that simply will not be noticed. Wrong – they will. A table – particularly a side table – need not be of conventional aspect or construction. A useful table to hold a reading lamp can be as simple as a pile of interestingly bound old encyclopedias or annuals placed next to a comfortable chair; other options come from the natural world, such as an interesting slab of wood or a large old pot with a plate glass top.

Although no one has ever yet attempted to upholster a table, there are decorative cloths which can make a table stand out in a room, and give it an entirely different look. On a round table, the cloth need not be floor length – in fact ready-made floor-length cloths these days look slightly old-fashioned, particularly those very neat ones with a matching frill skirting the base of the cloth. As with window treatments, frills and swagged bits now look distinctly excessive. Pieces of old textiles and old floor-length cloths can still work however, and this is an obvious way to display old textiles. They often look right precisely because they are not exactly the right length, and either show the feet of the table or trail onto the floor. In contrast, a short cloth, whether over a rectangular or a round table, looks very modern – particularly if it falls in points. As many old textiles tend toward the small, they could well work here.

and are often better when they do not. If you do have a pair of tables, the decorative interest lies in placing them at different points in the room, not along the same wall, or flanking a piece of furniture.

The variety of materials used in the design of different tables can be bewildering, and it is important to ensure that if you mix materials they will work together. The decorative use of paint should not be forgotten when selecting tables that will work with everything else in the room. Designer Frédéric Méchiche, who loves 18th-century furniture but, as he puts it, the simple furniture of the waiting room and the corridor rather than the grand pieces of the state rooms, often colours his antique tables and chairs a neutral, soft off-white. This allows him to see the lines without distraction – to really appreciate the furniture for itself.

It is not just a piece of 18th-century furniture that can benefit from this treatment: it also works on a less fine piece. A decently made table in an ugly wood or one that has been stained beyond any recognizable shade can often regain its dignity by being painted. Much of the 19th-century pine we lovingly strip back to the wood was, when first made, painted in a variety of colours – the Victorians would be horrified by our modern penchant for always going back to the wood. Many early pieces of furniture were painted in colours that ranged from the soft to the bright.

A group of very different elements – a painted pine dressing table, a distressed pine mirror, an Indian pottery light, a faux bamboo chair – are combined with a blue-and-white gingham cushion and Indian-inspired curtains (opposite above). The whole works because each element is light in style and appearance.

Purely for decoration: an ornate 19th-century shell decorative pattern in its octagonal glass-topped case has been made into a charming bedroom table – a device that could be used for any group of small fragile pieces, from silver boxes to antique toys (opposite below).

The simple but elegant lines of an English butler's tray stand out in a covered porch on a rustic floor of herringbone brick in Mississippi (above).

This fine example of a grand statement is in an East Hampton summer house (right). A group of pieces from vastly different places and periods are expertly brought together in a perfect illustration of using scale and proportion. There is a satisfying completeness to this table arrangement, the whole saved from pomposity by the ivy wreath that adds a witty note to the whole.

In antique dealer John Rosselli's barn (left), an 18th-century Portuguese chair is upholstered in a Robert Kime fabric. It sits in regal contrast to the painted wood walls, and the panel of old Dutch tiles.

This American sitting room is furnished with perfect early English and American antiques, including a fine Windsor chair of 1790 (below). The decoration is purposely plain in order to best display the furniture.

chairs

For anyone interested in furniture design, there is no more romantic piece of furniture than the chair. Its journey through history is the story of changing social patterns, and its changing shape a vivid reminder of how interior decoration and design accommodate and reflect the fashion and modes of the day. Widely illustrated in classical art and in painted frescos, and on stone stele, pottery jars and vases, the chair was the first piece of furniture to be depicted as an object of beauty as opposed to an object of pure function. Throughout history seats have always been used to denote status – or the lack of it – with particular types of chair and stool reserved for specific groups. The height; the decoration; whether it is to be with or without arms, with or without upholstery – these seemingly minor points have had a significance which go beyond the practical role of the chair.

There have also always been chairs which, in their very making, were perceived as far more than mere pieces of furniture – artists and craftsmen seem to have delighted in using the basic shape to indulge their finest

A quirky combination of furniture can be very successful. Here a 19th-century leather-covered armchair is placed next to a log stool made in the distinctive style of the Adirondacks (below top right).

In the Paris apartment of a discerning collector stand two 1940's wrought-iron chairs designed by André Arbus (below right). Their angular lines are emphasized by the 18th-century wooden panelling.

flights of design fancy – think of the very different, but equally original. chairs designed by craftsmen such as William Kent, Thomas Sheraton (1751-1806) and Le Corbusier (1887-1965).

It was during the 17th and 18th centuries – particularly in France, and especially during the reigns of the three kings named Louis – that chairs were first designed to encompass many different functions. There were chairs for eating, chairs for working and reading, and importantly, chairs simply for conversation. Stuffed chairs with soft cushions that made reading and relaxing a pleasure became popular at this time, reflecting a new concern, in some echelons of society, with comfort and leisure.

In France – always a leader in the nebulous pleasures of convenience and style – there had for some time been two kinds of chair: *chaises meublants* and *chaises courantes*. The former remained in fixed positions in the room (usually against a wall, and so the back remained undecorated); while the latter were placed where needed, and were light and portable.

This figurative balloon chair with its 18th-century lines (right) was possibly made for the Metropolitan Opera House in New York.

A cane chair painted in green-grey against a green-grey wooden background is a soothing combination (below).

Such an attention-seeking chair needs no other background than this fine panelling and floor (below centre).

In artist Frank Faulkner's loft, a gilded Gothic chair is pointedly set against a pointilliste background created from the discarded paint-spattered plywood sections of his studio floor (below right).

An Eastern wooden chair with almost classical Greek lines, cushioned in mattress ticking, stands conveniently close to the bookshelves (bottom).

A chair, more than any other piece of furniture, should be looked at dispassionately for its shape and decorative qualities alone. As with so many items of furniture, often not enough thought is given to the way a chair looks on its own, as an object. When you have registered that, then it can be thought about in a specific context: how well it will mix with, and tie together, the other things in that room, and also whether anything about the chair itself – colour, decoration, upholstery – will have to be changed.

If you think of chairs as shapes, you will see that they can be used as important decorative tools – accents to fill a blank space, or to work

By the end of the Victorian era, as evidenced by innumerable paintings and photographs, many drawing rooms were so full of chairs, tables, and other evidently essential whatnots that avoiding them must have been more like negotiating an obstacle course than crossing a room.

When using chairs in decorative schemes today, the most important thing to remember is the chairs in any room do not have to be part of a set. In fact, many decorators prefer that there are not even any matching pairs – in the same way they abhor pairs of lamps, especially those used either end of a shelf or table.

with other disparate elements of a room. Scale, as with every aspect of successful interior design and decoration, is what is important. A fragile spindly side chair would obviously be dwarfed and look glaringly out of place if surrounded by monumental furniture and large pictures. Equally, a heavy oak settle would not look right nestling among filigree furniture of spider's-web charm. A good chair is in many ways like a sculpture, and every part has its own charm. The curve of a chair leg, the intricate carving of a back, the decoration of an arm – all of these elements reward further study.

Different chairs are often used in a group, and there should be a link to bind them together. Rounded-back chairs, for instance, always work together, whatever the materials and whatever their size, although it is best if they are all roughly the same height. What a chair is made from can also be the connecting factor: something solid like oak or pine, or more decorative such as bamboo or papier mâché. Upholstered chairs require thought on the right choice of fabric for the shape – an armless bedroom chair covered in an oversized, overloud abstract print looks worryingly out of place; the same chair covered in a more regular, smaller design will

The lines of a skinny metal framed chair (left) in a sunny porch are accentuated by the solid silhouette of the up-ended terracotta pots.

Bamboo legs and single-strip webbing arms ensure this campaign chair is light enough to be portable (below left). It is draped with a Moroccan rug.

The carved back on this soft-green painted wooden chair with woven webbing seat represents a military trophy (below centre).

A chair designed by Carlo Bugatti in Italy in the late 19th century is set against the 18th-century panelled walls of a Paris apartment (below).

Upholstered in contemporary but classical design, this comfortable 19th-century chair is set next to a large Eastern metal pot (bottom).

immediately look desirable. It is a question of scale – of the design of the fabric to the shape and size of the chair, and also the scale of the chair itself. As London-based interior designer Alidad says, 'It is not so much a question of what fabrics you put on upholstered furniture – if the scale of the pieces you are using is wrong then no covers in the world will save them.'

The upholstery is incredibly important in a room of mixed styles. Firstly, look at the shape of a chair and then think about how it would be best upholstered or cushioned. When using chairs of different shapes, styles and periods,

sometimes, but not always, the same design and shade of an upholstery fabric will unify them all; sometimes they will need several different patterns but all in the same colour tones. There are some patterns, designs and fabrics that have a history, that have become classics in the sense of being universally accepted and acceptable, and these can provide a strong link when bringing together different designs. Try the so-called Regency stripes; woollen checks; traditional gingham in candy-floss colours; small sprigged flowers; plain unbleached calico; woollen crewel work; or dark 16th-century damask designs –

because of their universal appeal these designs do not detract from the shape of different chairs and indeed unify them in a contemporary way.

When combining styles and periods, one of the most important things is not to take the obvious view when considering the use of a piece of furniture. When you look at a chair, do you only see it as something to be sat on? If so, think again. There are so many small decorative chairs around and many of them can be used to hold books, towels, lights, flowers. They are often beautiful pieces in their own right and using them in this way makes them appreciated, and, more important, really looked at.

This calm blue-and-white corner is in a house in Normandy (below). An easy chair has been transformed with tie-on loose covers and bolsters in old blue-and-white striped fabric. An eclectic arrangement of objects, including part of an old door, part of a balustrade and decorative white painted frames, are used as ornament in their own right.

An armchair covered in natural weave is placed beside a plaster table and dominated by an antique white painted wooden capstan leaning against the corner wall (below).

The clear light of the south illuminates a French sitting room (right), where a classical sofa sits beside a stripped 18th-century chair, the two united by being upholstered in simple cream linen covers. The tones of the old floor are taken up by the cushion and the wooden chair.

In an East Hampton beach house (left), a cane chair is upholstered in large soft cushions in a large scale design and surrounded with plants to make a wind-free summer room.

A simple seating arrangement in a Manhattan loft (above), where a carved chair of white painted wood with leather seat sits in front of a tall window hung with a cream holland blind and a curtain made of unlined cotton and tied with string, frayed at the ends.

This interesting conjunction of a contemporary, sophisticated armchair beside a quirky Indian horn and metal table with a combination of interesting objects was arranged by Vicente Wolf (below).

Christopher Gibbs uses a palette of colour and pattern to blend chair, desk and table (below). The colour of the distinctive William Morris wallpaper and the painted table are extremely harmonious with the mellow leather chair.

Even miniature chairs have their place in a decorative scheme. These two antique pieces in a conversational pairing beside the fire add a witty note in Christopher Hodsoll's London drawing room (below).

Robert Kime combines textures and patterns in a masterful manner (above). Here, an antique cane chair is placed against a dark screen which frames it.

This antique armchair is covered in an almost self-coloured stripe that, although contemporary, is exactly the right scale for the chair (right).

Only someone with the taste and confidence of Christopher Gibbs would think of putting these two chairs – each very different – and soft-shaded standard lamp in front of a screen papered in such a delicate design (opposite). And it works.

Chairs are decorative objects in their own right (clockwise from left): a chair made by Christopher Hodsoll is covered in wonderful lipstick pink leather; the pink is emphasized by the antique carpet. A pair of stools is reminiscent of Greek X-form stools. In a Tuscan farmhouse, a dramatic horn chair with yellow striped seat needs no other embellishment. An antique faux bamboo chair has been unusually, and successfully, covered in a French toile de Jouy design. Decorator Prue Lane has made a chair of classical design into something striking using a bold contemporary blue-and-white check against a glazed celadon green wall.

Forties' dining chairs in strong toned leather (left) are set against original green *boiserie* in an 18th-century Paris apartment.

An 18th-century chair is upholstered in severe grey and painted (above), allowing the lines to show without distraction.

Eccentric and original, this parchment chair designed by Carlo Bugatti in the late 19th century needs no additions (above).

A metal dining chair stands next to a Directoire charcoal burner (right), against a distressed wall of several layers of blue.

sofas and day beds

The shape of a sofa or day bed can vary enormously. There are those that are elegant – all light and lithe lines – and then there are those that are cumbersome, back-breaking, tortured shapes which, overstuffed and often over-buttoned, are good for nothing except a perverse cat to sit on. But when the shape is right – a basic simple form with the right depth of seat and height of back – a sofa can be a most pleasant addition to a room. Instead of a conventional design, substitute an old bench, a Scandinavian painted settle, or perhaps a Provençal caned seat. Any day bed or chaise longue, or even a sleigh bed, with the addition of bolsters and cushions, can be used either for sitting or sleeping.

A meeting of centuries: sitting on the original 18th-century parquet floor, and set against the original wooden panelling (left), is a set of metal chairs and sofa designed in the 1940s, with a distinctly 20th-century painting hung above.

Frédéric Méchiche has no fears about combining periods (below). In his Paris drawing room he successfully surrounds an 18th-century settee with various pieces from the 20th century – a modern metal frame and canvas chair, two small circular laminated tables, and chrome angle lamps.

A metal-framed campaign bed is used as a day bed (opposite). Upholstered with comfortable seat cushions, it is placed against some old green-stained shutters that are used as a screen. Beside it is a table of black marble on an iron base, and the walls are decorated with an eclectic selection, covering different continents and cultures, of plaster seals, a laurel wreath and two African masks.

This wooden-framed sofa in Manhattan (above) has been made part of a pleasing composition which combines contrasting textures and materials, like the paisley shawl draped over the back, the soft white cotton cushions and a small rectangular table in front holding an antique model.

One of the most successful ways to show off period furniture is to put it in a contemporary setting so the clean lines of floors, walls and windows will point out, not detract, from the group (right).

A cupboard can be – as it once was – a showcase for objects as well as textiles and linens. This painted early French armoire (left) displays a collection of jugs and porcelain as well as some pieces of antique textiles.

In many cases the top of the cupboard is too good an area to leave empty. As well as correcting the proportions of the piece in relation to the rest of the room, it can be used as a display shelf for large striking pieces, drawing the eye upwards (below and right). A simple cupboard washed green has above it a single piece of celadon coloured ceramic which seems at one with the cupboard (below). A washed-white Gothic-influenced cupboard (right) acts as a display shelf for an assorted selection of ceramics, blue and white, offset by cream glazed pots.

cupboards

Cupboards have always been important pieces of furniture in a household. Often elaborate in design and richly painted and gilded, they were intended not only to store various goods but also to display the householder's collection of valuable plate (it was important for this to be seen, as it was a good measure of an individual's wealth). The cupboard itself was designed not only to reflect the prestige of its contents, but also the significance of its owner. By the 17th century, it was very often the grandest piece of furniture in the room, by this time displaying rarities, curiosities and treasured possessions as well as plate. As such it was often ornamented and decorated in a rich manner.

There is a physical weight and stature to a cupboard or sideboard that cannot be denied and it should be treated either as a central focus or matched in weight and density by the other furnishings. Rooms often look overpowered if they contain one relatively large cupboard and everything else is comparatively small. When

A handsome antique Eastern lacquered cupboard is an appropriate platform for a collection of Eastern art (top).

The curved lines of an antique corner cupboard show off the 18th-century ceramic water urn (above). The dark antique chair with its striking striped cover is in sharp contrast.

The role of a bookcase does not end with the housing of books: the top of a bookcase can be a platform for adjusting the proportions and scale of a room. Group together large pieces of ceramics, or a collection of small sculpture or busts - anything which takes the eye upwards and which links the walls to the ceiling.

The books themselves within the case are also an important element of a decorated room. It is not just a cliché; books really do furnish a room. A room without any books can have a slightly unreal air about it. Like flowers, books personalize and give to a room an instantly friendly air. Many of them are also, importantly, a decorative feature in themselves: their colours, their bindings and jackets, even their shapes, make them objects of desire. Books need not, and indeed should not, be confined only to bookshelves and bookcases. Books look well piled on tables (not too symmetrically), on the floor, even up a staircase.

you enter a room your eye always seeks out an architectural focus, but there is not always one to be found. In a small room without any focal point – for that matter, in any sized room without any architectural point of attention such as a fireplace or striking windows – a large piece of furniture such as a cupboard or a bookcase can create a focus where none existed before.

Bookcases, with their symbiotic association with books and the pleasure of reading, are emotive pieces of furniture. Books themselves, with their variety of texture, can be better than the most luxurious fabric or most expensive wallpaper as a background for objects, and should be used as such. So a bookcase, while of course being used primarily to hold and display books, can also in most cases be used as a backdrop for other pieces: small sculptures, pictures, objects. The regular shapes of books contrasting with the rounded forms of pottery or porcelain is particularly pleasing.

In this Tuscan house, the cupboard is used as the ultimate display case (opposite above and below). Painted a dramatic deep red, and standing against a saffron wall, the shelves are crammed with things – personal things, pretty pieces, postcards, photographs, pictures and books. Above the cupboard are some pieces of antique architectural instruments – a reminder of the architect owner's profession.

The old armoire in a Provençal house is painted white, with the panels lined with fabric (left above). Contrasting with this are the blue striped walls, hand-painted by the house's owner, the artist Giorgio Silvagni, as is the lampshade of the desk lamp. The table is covered with a quilt.

A painted pine linen cupboard displays a collection of glazed urns and pots (left) and a candelabra made of bayonets. An empty frame draws the pieces together.

Olive green against the terracotta coloured walls, a huge old armoire is a simple and handsome object in its own right, and needs no additional ornament save two baskets of dried flowers (above).

desks, bureaux and chests of drawers

A desk can be so much more than a piece of furniture. With its intimations of learning and creative imagination it is in a way an object to which people are drawn as well as a repository of sometime secrets lost perhaps in a hidden compartment or drawer. As with the cupboard, the desk developed from a functional item – a simple surface on which to write – into an

Animal heaven: Indian figures of a dog and a cow stand commandingly beneath a painting of ruminating cattle (far left).

No decorator or designer can resist the opportunities offered by the inviting flat surface of a desk. This perfect neoclassical composition (left) is based around a fine Empire desk and chair.

A severe, striking arrangement is set on a plain chest in front of a holland-covered window which acts as an opaque background (below left).

A fine carved antique Italian bureau (above) is made more striking with the choice of objects displayed upon it – the head of a fat cherub and a Chinese vase.

White combines with white for a unifying aesthetic (above): on top of a apothecary's chest are white vases and jugs and a glass bell jar against an old painting.

important piece of furniture, to be admired and displayed. Perhaps for these reasons, the desk has often been made the vehicle for flights of craftsmen's creative fancy – often carved, decorated, ornamented and embellished.

This strength of character also means that a desk must be considered in the general scheme of decoration and not sidelined. Useful in a room where scale is a consideration, a desk adds mass and can be a focus where none exists. A

tall desk, which often has a varied assortment of shelves, niches and pigeonholes, is also a natural background for displaying pieces – particularly collections of things miniature and minute, things which are precious to their owner.

Another equally substantial and useful piece of furniture, that we know today as a chest of drawers, developed from the innovative 17th-century practice of adding a drawer beneath a storage chest. By the Restoration, the whole chest was often taken up with drawers, and these continued to be made until the Georgian period. It was at this time that the flat-fronted, distinctive chest-of-drawers became popular, and it has remained so until our own time.

A bright blue and terracotta painted chest of drawers stands out against more muted but complementary blue-stained walls (above right).

A pleasing arrangement utilizes the vertical and horizontal (above). To break up any severity, an amassed group of objects extends the eye upwards.

Fabrics

When you use old textiles, they speak of the creative ability and imagination of the people who made them, the skill and the inspiration behind the designs. Antique hand-woven or hand-printed materials are unique – each piece not only charming in its own right, but a chronicle of other times and fashions. Do not reject scraps or even off-cuts – they can be used to cover a cushion, border a curtain or simply draped over the end of a bed.

There are so many different patterns on the textiles and pictures in this room in East Hampton (left), but they all work together because they share a tradition of Eastern motif and design.

An old piece of paisley textile has been used to make a bolster exactly the length of one angle of the window seat (above). Two small pictures propped against the ledge draw attention to the cushion as well as to each other.

curtains and blinds

From medieval times until around the 17th century textiles were often considered more significant than the furniture around them. Tapestries, bed hangings and curtains were the stuff of importance and status as well as cost; wall and bed hangings in particular were often, in inventories of the day, minutely described and itemized. Textiles simultaneously brought warmth, decoration and grandeur to bare cold interiors. The production of such textiles became a prosperous and vibrant pan-European industry: from the 12th century Italy produced rich silks, and by the 14th century opulent velvets were woven in cities like Genoa, Florence and Milan. In France by the 17th century, there were woven silks, taffeta brocades and satins from the weavers of Lyons; and a century later printed and glazed cottons and linens were being produced throughout Europe.

Early curtains were simple affairs – a piece of fabric attached to a rod or hung on hooks to add a degree of draught exclusion combined with some light allowance. By the 17th century, curtains had become far more elaborate, often being designed to match costly bed drapes. Although the trend today is towards simpler curtains, this does not mean the formal curtain is dead – far from it. Curtains of all types are still very necessary; as well as being dramatic decorative elements in their own right, they are an admirable way of pulling a room together. It is the word 'simple' which is important. A room where all the elements are different and disparate would not react well to elaborate drapes and swagged curtains.

Appropriate with most contemporary furniture would be a treatment in the spirit of the Regency, with curtains in a soft fabric draped over a pole in loose asymmetrical swags. Rooms furnished in different styles can be unified by using the same blinds throughout the house, either fabric, venetian, light split-cane or other wood. Large patterns on curtains do not work well in a room which combines many different elements and styles. Such designs call too much attention to themselves, detracting from the harmony of a carefully thought-out arrangement. For emphasis, instead of overscaled patterns, use bold trimmings like braid or fringing.

This London drawing room is L-shaped, and the tail of L is used as a study (below). A pair of imposing curtains, complete with pelmet and tassels, mark the different functions of the room. Note the placing of the two old leather chairs, which stand like attendants to the sanctum within.

In a bedroom in which the bathroom is very much en suite (left), the two areas are differentiated with a pair of simple curtains on a pole across the entrance.

Robert Kime uses crewel work for curtains at a window beside a rustic table filled with interesting objects (below).

The kitchen in this house opens directly into the dining room. The dramatic, heavy curtains made from one of owner Christopher Hodsoll's own textiles, both close off any evidence of the kitchen and link the other areas of the dining room together (above and left).

In a potentially dark dining room, antique panels of lace, which have been made into roller blinds, are hung at different heights (far left). There are no other curtains, only shutters.

soft furnishings

Textiles are vitally important to the finish of a room. They add texture, depth and interest and give a room an inherent comfort that cannot be achieved through hard surfaces alone. Today we are, literally, spoiled for choice in textiles, so much so that in many interiors, the excess of choice seems to invite a lazy way of using what there is available. And this is not only a shame but it also leads to bad interior decoration. Material, when it is imaginatively and skilfully employed, can make a room outstanding. But when used unwisely it can ruin any effect, no matter how carefully planned. So think before you choose a fabric.

The way you cover a chair, sofa or bed affects everything about the piece of furniture. With the right material and the right design you can enhance, spotlight, disguise, and old or unusual textiles can take a leading role here. They can be used not just for curtains but as all manner of soft

Christophe Gollut is a collector of textiles and displays them everywhere. Here a narrow, bordered strip of an antique textile is folded informally over the back and seat of a 19th-century armchair (above).

A small cloakroom has been lined with pleated modern fabric in a traditional design that not only gives the room a warm feeling, but also acts as a foil for the inlaid Indian mirror and the picture of an equally ornate courtier (above right).

In Alidad's library, some of his large collection of antique textiles are folded in rich layers over the back of a comfortable reading chair, where they can be easily appreciated (right).

furnishings and decorative touches. Old shawls in a traditional paisley pattern, or embroidered or printed silk or cotton, can be used to cover a modern (or old) chair – either completely enveloping it, or draped or folded over the back or seat. Designer Alidad, for example, takes three, four or five old textiles, folds them and layers them over the back of a chair so each pattern leads to another. Old textiles are infinitely obliging – if they are torn, marked or otherwise damaged they can be arranged so that the best part shows. They can be changed with the seasons – use lightweight linens, cottons and silks in warm weather, and wool, brocade and woven pieces, even tapestry and needlepoint, when winter comes.

In the bedroom they can be made into decorative or sham pillow, or used on the bed itself, folded at one end of the bed in a rectangular or triangular shape. Collectors of quilts often use two or three on the same bed, perhaps a quilted floral print set off by a traditional square design at the bottom of the bed. Strips of lace or embroidered ribbon can also be

In one small corner of Alidad's drawing room (above), the club fender is covered in one old textile and then draped with another, and a stool beside the fire is covered with old velvet with a small scrap of another antique piece stitched across the top.

In the cobbled floor living room of a house in Provence, a piece of old Bargello-type tapestry is draped over the front of the large stone fireplace (far left). Other pieces of fabric are piled in a basket at one side of the fire.

An antique textile is not only displayed to its best advantage but also cleverly used by Christopher Gibbs to cover an out-of-proportion dead space under a window (left). The whole area has become a decorative feature instead of a lost space.

A strong colour and design of cloth are used on a round table to tie in with the rich-coloured shelves and the stencilled and painted wall (far left).

A red-painted stool at a faux bamboo table next to a faux bamboo folding chair brighten a corner in East Hampton (left).

used to edge a plain sheet or bed cover. Every time you use a piece of textile in this way you add to the depth of the room. It is good for any textiles – old and new – to be seen and to be admired. A door that is perpetually open, for example, is a good easel for a scrap of fabric.

The smallest and largest of pieces can be used to good effect over patterned pieces – a tapestry stool, a damask chair. Over tables they can either drop to the floor or half way down, sometimes over a lower cloth, sometimes, if there are interesting legs on the table, showing off the legs. A long table can have a long strip of

textile on it – either running down the centre as a runner or covering the whole space as a short cloth in the same way that carpets were used in the 17th century.

If using modern fabrics on old furniture it is more scale that counts than the pattern itself, for if the scale is wrong, nothing else will work. Do not automatically select a new fabric in a traditional design when covering an old piece. Much more interesting is to find a modern design which shows up the lines of the chair or sofa, and which will highlight the relationship between old and new.

In this study in black and white, a low black lacquered chair is covered, almost casually, with plain cream calico that is simply tied on around the legs and back (above). A striking plaster nautilus shell stands on the table beside.

So simple and yet so comfortable: a long sofa has been covered in plain white material, and comfortable, squashy cushions have been added (right). The relaxed seating contrasts favourably with the purity of the 18th-century ceramics.

Against brilliant jade-green walls, a plain neutrally coloured sofa is liberally coated with textiles ranging from leopard skin to toile de Jouy, and blue-and-white striped cushions (opposite). George Washington serenely surveys the scene.

cushions

Cushions are the final touch. Here a white-painted wooden seat, Eastern in influence, is covered in white self-striped fabric with knotted bolsters in a toning stripe (above). What brings it alive, however, is the rectangular kilim cushion at the back of the seat.

Cushions made from pieces of old textiles make any sofa appear even more inviting and comfortable in Robert Kime's Wiltshire house (above right top and centre).

A woven needlework cushion contrasts interestingly with the printed cover of Alidad's sofa (above right bottom).

Cushions are an integral part of any decorative scheme – but only if they are the right cushions. They can add necessary pattern and design to a room without overwhelming it, but they are less successful when they are made in too strident or too aggressively modern a fabric – classical new or subtle old look best. Indeed, according to designer Robert Kime, there is no contest – cushions should always be made from old textiles.

These textiles do not have to cost much, and often do not even have to be bought. Any linen cupboard will yield pieces which, although at first sight unlikely, can be used for cushions. Small pieces can be centred as panels on toning background fabric, or made into a border on a plain material. Old lace, although less fashionable than it was, is worth keeping to sew onto a bedroom pillow – preferably without the addition of a frill.

The sofa and cushions in Alidad's library are literally an in-depth study of using cushions decoratively (above right). Three deep, they climb the sofa back – which itself is draped in a rug – to meet the strong design of the stencilled wall above.

Lars Bolander here uses cushions both as decoration in themselves and also as a device linking the set of unframed pictures on the wall above to the seating beneath (right). The pictures have gold tones within them, and the pale gold cushions are graded in size, taking the eye smoothly upward.

Three details of Alidad's mixture of textiles and cushions (above top), and some of Robert Kime's collection of antique cushions (above centre and bottom), demonstrate how design and pattern can be mixed with insouciance.

A wider view of one of the sofas in Robert Kime's drawing room (left) shows how old tapestry, woven and printed cushions can be viewed both for their individual beauty and also for the beauty and colour of the designs en masse.

wall hangings

In the Middle Ages, when a noble or particularly wealthy household travelled between estates, the woven tapestry wall hangings travelled with them to provide both instant decoration and comfort at journey's end. Wall hangings were the first way in which textiles were employed, and although they are not much used now in the traditional form of tapestries and specially woven panels, textiles are once again being hung on walls for decoration. Suspended either as a single or double panel, or perhaps as a small or fragmented piece of fabric fastened behind sheets of clear glass or perspex and fixed on the wall, making a frame within a frame, they are seen as a more unusual alternative to a picture.

Other than for decoration, the reasons for which hangings were first employed – warmth and insulation – still apply, and to that end fabric can also of course be used around the entire room, interlined, battened and stapled in place, and then finished with tape or binding. Fabric used like this, as well as adding warmth gives definite atmosphere to a room and is

Christophe Gollut loves and collects lengths of antique textiles. Here, he hangs a particularly rare and beautiful length over the door which leads into his dining room, not only displaying it to best effect, but also defining the entrance to the room beyond (above).

In his drawing room too, Gollut uses textiles wherever he can (left). On the sofa there are cushions covered in different antique fabrics and a strongly coloured piece of tapestry hangs on a door which no longer leads anywhere. The door itself is bordered by a surround of more tapestry. Note how the painted screen relates in height to the door textiles, so that neither of them is left floating in mid-air.

A wall hanging is tied into the overall scheme of this room (left) by the printed cloth on the table, which is in many of the same tones.

In a Mississippi plantation house (below left) an American Federal chair is put beside an American marble-topped console table above which is a strong American hanging.

An antique tapestry is seen at its best behind a massive refectory table (above). Candlesticks, figures, ceramics and bronzes on the floor are used to correct the scale and take the eye from table to tapestry.

In less sure hands this profusion of textiles and patterns might not work (right), but Alidad has selected the right pieces so that the antique textiles on the door and wall work with everything else.

an all-embracing background for a multitude of dissimilar periods. Like the right paint colour, textiles on the wall, whether old or new, can be used to pull together disparate objects and styles. When choosing a fabric for this treatment you can either choose plain or patterned. If you opt for plain, choose a textured finish – perhaps hessian (which is making a style comeback), linen or canvas. If choosing a patterned design, pick one that does not have too many different colours within it, and also one that either through design or texture has a certain subtlety and depth. Old – and new – textiles can also be displayed by hanging them, as both Alidad and Christophe Gollut do, over a tall door.

Objects and Ornaments

This is a fantastic set piece if ever there was one, and immensely successful (above and opposite). Lars Bolander's dining room in West Palm Beach is a symphony of texture – wood, plaster, ceramics and silver – and colour. Harmonious neutrals predominate.

Little things give such pleasure. It is those – the details, rather than the large set pieces – that create the atmosphere in a room. Lars Bolander says it is the way you put things together, rather than the things themselves. Christopher Gibbs says it is like knitting – a rather intricate weaving that makes many single strands into a cohesive whole. Anything and everything can be used: there is only one criteria – that it is something which you really like and want to have around you.

The pale delicacy of this collection of fine 18th-century porcelain and bibelots (left) is thrown into sharp relief in an old cupboard left in its original, unrestored state in Frédéric Méchiche's country house in southern France.

ceramics and china

These black decorated pieces were made as discreet symbols of mourning after the executions of Louis XVI and Marie Antoinette (above right).

The delight in this display is in the curves of the stacked plates peering out from a round painted commode (right).

In Robert Kime's kitchen (far right), decorative painted pottery and china objects and plates, all very different, are grouped together. The differences in density and shape between the objects and the similarity in colour unites the group.

It is the appreciation of the smallest of things – like ceramics – which can make a room or a corner. For many people ceramics and china are the easiest things to collect – something indeed which is collected almost subconsciously, for from childhood there are the must-have groups of china animals, little houses, or doll's house-size cups and saucers. From that point it is easy enough to keep on looking, keep on finding, keep on acquiring until, almost before you know it, you have a collection of china.

The joys of collecting china are various: firstly it can be as cheap a pastime – or as expensive – as you desire, with subjects ranging from hand-thrown bowls, teapots or egg cups to precious rare porcelain.

In his drawing room, Robert Kime combines two small fine pieces of blue-and-white china – a vase and a bowl – with an assortment of other objects and pictures on a mantelpiece to make a text-book example of how to put together seemingly unrelated objects (left).

Antiques dealer Christopher Gibbs is known for his ability to achieve harmony and proportion in his arrangements. Here he places three different but equally delicate pieces of decorative blue-and-white china against a forthright back-ground of painted columns (right).

In this Provençal home glazed urns and pots and a candelabra made from old bayonets sit on a painted pine linen cup-board (left). The group is pulled together by being placed within an empty frame.

An arrangement by Christopher Hodsoll renders a rare and beautiful jar even more beautiful by placing it in front of an antique mirror whose aged glass and creamy backing reflect the same milky blue tones as the jar (right). The miniature column and ceramic figure complete the group.

Secondly there is the pleasure of the shapes – the curve of a jug, the sphere of a bowl. Then there is such a wealth of decoration, with designs that range from quite primitive patterns to highly sophisticated, detailed designs. And finally there are the colours, pigments and glazes – the latter demonstrating techniques of often intense virtuosity.

Success in displaying a collection of china has much to do with the way in which it is presented – if it is set against a wall, for example, make sure that the background works with what is in front of it. Instead of setting the collection in context, so to speak, use a contrast of period and of texture and colour. A certain irreverence is required, but then that goes

for decorating with antiques generally. A collection of obviously Victorian jugs, for example, will look all the more interesting against shiny metal or glass or a strong, vibrant colour.

With any collection of china, large or small, it is important that it is well lit, whether by natural or artificial light. Daylight flatters china, but if it is in short supply a collection can be lit with specific accent lights or up-lighting. The flicker of candlelight is particularly effective in high-lighting the beauty of ceramics, and decorative candlesticks can often be effectively woven into a collection of china. The important thing is to form a composition that works in relation to the rest of the room.

silver and glass

No matter what silver or glass you have, it is far more striking when two or more pieces are displayed together. More is more might be the rule here. It does not seem to matter about mixing styles and periods, sizes and shapes. Elaborate cut glass can sit next to plain, and even small pots can be placed beside tall fluted Victorian celery glasses. Well-polished silver in different shapes or periods grouped also work. Give a display contrast in height and more than one dimension; a flat silver-framed mirror is good behind silver pots, boxes and cream jugs. Silver containers, whether or not they were designed for the purpose, look even better with flowers in them. The more formal the piece, the more rural or informal the arrangement can be.

This traditional way of displaying glass – setting simple pieces of different shapes and sizes against a window – is still one of the most effective way of showing a collection's clear beauty (below).

A stunning grouping of silver uses pieces from different periods, united by the simplicity of the painted wooden shelves, and tied together by the judicious addition of paintings and china (opposite).

All silver and glass looks at its best when grouped closely together, not spaced out, as these three good examples demonstrate (above).

Art glass figures from the 1940s of the finest quality need no decorative device to show them off, other than the simplest of glass shelving (right).

single objects

There are few people who do not own at least one or two decorative objects, but it can be very difficult to display one object in a room that has other focuses. The piece must either stand alone – which should only happen if it is arresting in design – or connect in some way with another piece or group in the room; consider unusual combinations and striking conjunctions with anything else in the same area.

Often the most interesting things in a room are the objects that have been placed there for pure pleasure – things which have no relation to the function or overall scheme of that room. Their interest might lie in their shape or design or often the now obsolete purpose for which they were originally used. Many antiques fall into this category – the curious weighing scales, a huge brass weight, an early piece of industrial technology, a fragment of another world – or something else, well turned or carved, that has

This unusual model of a head rises almost pillar-like upon its pediment of leather-bound books (above).

A giant antique copper urn is placed in the brick floor of a house in Italy (below). The contrast of textures between plaster, brick and metal is immensely satisfying.

In a Swedish-influenced house in East Hampton a wooden decoy duck roosts in an iron heart attached by a chain to one of the decoratively painted beams and rafters (above right).

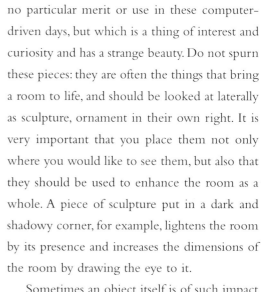

no particular merit or use in these computer-driven days, but which is a thing of interest and curiosity and has a strange beauty. Do not spurn these pieces: they are often the things that bring a room to life, and should be looked at laterally as sculpture, ornament in their own right. It is very important that you place them not only where you would like to see them, but also that they should be used to enhance the room as a whole. A piece of sculpture put in a dark and shadowy corner, for example, lightens the room by its presence and increases the dimensions of the room by drawing the eye to it.

Sometimes an object itself is of such impact that nothing else could work with it, or it might be of such a size that nothing could balance it in scale. Obviously if it is rare or a major work of art, it must stand alone. If it does, then its background and surroundings must enhance it and not fight against it.

An antique birdcage in the form of a house is raised on a stand in front of a window so that the light can flood through the structure (right).

An 18th-century porcelain clock stands before a heavily distressed plaster wall. The delicacy of the clock is thrown into relief by the texture of the wall (below left top).

On a rustic wooden wall shelf stands an early American pottery jug (below left bottom). The white brick wall is a clean and effective foil.

A wooden model of an early sailing ship is secured above the large mantlepiece in this American kitchen (below). The eye is drawn upwards to the boat and its details.

collections

We are all to a greater or lesser extent collectors at heart and, even more, we are all makers of collections. Childhood trawls for precious shells, stones and birds' eggs instill in us a liking of the idea of collecting things – and more things. Collections should not be hidden away in boxes and cupboards. They should be out there, displayed and giving a room spirit.

In any room a cohesive collection will look better than a just a few scattered objects. But a collection need not be valuable, fragile or even large. What a collection is a grouping – a statement. Often people have collections without even knowing it: several things made from the same material, several depictions of the same subject.

Although these African masks in a Paris flat are strong on their own, they are even stronger when two or more are grouped together (left).

When showing primitive or ethnic pieces together (right), they are seen to best advantage when they are displayed as sculptural forms in their own right.

A group can work even if the pieces are from different sources as long there is a spatial connection (above). A metal piece by 1940's designer André Arbus is grouped with masks and votive figures in front of a Chinese painting hung over a mirror.

This conjunction between very different pieces of widely varying provenance, including a Picasso ceramic on the wall, proves undeniably that Frédéric Méchiche has an unmatched sense of shape and form (right).

Frédéric Méchiche positively enjoys
putting together pieces with different
pasts (top). A restored 14th-century jar sits
beside dishes made in the 1960s. Behind is
a 1st-century Roman torso.

With the archeological finds displayed
with their original identifying labels
still intact (above), Robert Kime's drawing
room table exudes the air of a small
private museum.

A collection is always, or should be, immediately recognizable as such and, equally immediately, a comment on your personality and taste. It can be as large or as minute as your pocket and your interest will allow. We do not use the term 'collection' here in the sense of a group painstakingly brought together by someone who has left no stone unturned to find the last, the missing piece – for our purposes, a collection is simply a group of things brought together for any number of different reasons. They may be brought together because of a link in subject, colour, shape or texture – either the similarities of these qualities or their contrasts.

Any collection is after all only a group of things that have some connection, however tenuous that connection may be. They may perhaps be all of one colour, bright blue or yellow, or – equally strong – in a monochrome like black or white. They may be all one subject: soldiers, suns, hippopotami. Perhaps they are all one material – wood, bronze, terracotta – or they may all be one art form – bronzes, plaster heads, oil paintings or embroidered samplers. Their common currency might even be that they are all the same shape – spheres, triangles, cubes. Or there may be a theme to the collection – nautical, equestrian, rural.

It may even be that all the various objects have in common is that they are an eclectic group of things which happen to look well together when placed in conjunction with each other. Like a convivial group at a party,

John Rosselli is a true collector, and in his New Jersey home, he displays many of his best finds in clever groups that show each piece, separately and together, to its best advantage. Blue-and-white china in a formal arrangement uses contrast of shape to make the picture (left).

Blue-and-white plates and chargers are also grouped in the corner of a room, running continuously from one wall to the other (above). They seamlessly overlap a central red and gold Chinese mirror, the display uninterrupted because of the reflection of the adjoining wall.

they do not all have to be dressed in the same style of clothes or be of the same height, they must simply have a pleasing appearance when standing together. Many of the best collections in fact do not at first appear to have an obvious outward link, but instead have an inward link or something more subtle, such as pattern or texture, which contrasts with and forms a connection with the other pieces in the group. In these instances mass and proportion come very much into the equation.

Working on the arrangement and display of a collection of small-scale objects sometimes helps to work out how best to arrange the proportions of the larger pieces in a room, such as the furniture, for the balance and harmony of proportion is constant whether the pieces are large or small. It is a useful exercise to arrange objects on a table; if you place an object of a certain height, for example, it is easy to see what else might go beside it. A tall and thin object needs other fatter, rounder things with it, but of a certain height. Equally, a squatter, rounder object cannot be grouped with things that are even squatter. It is an easy matter to then apply these lessons in scale to the general furniture and furnishings. There must be a discipline in displaying any sort of collection, and the more haphazard in

Simplicity can also be obtained by a minor weeding out of objects. In some cases, if you have a lot of one sort of thing in a particular collection, the pieces might look better displayed as two coherent groups, sited in different places in the room – each group balancing out the other. The eye must be able to distinguish between and appreciate individual objects even when they are seen in a massed group. Discipline is needed. It is the ability to subtract rather than to add that makes the art of decorating dependent on an instinctive knowledge of popular mathematics.

It is, in fact, often better, especially with a large collection of pieces which need to be displayed on flat surfaces, to actually remove a number of the pieces and store them out of sight for a while. Rather, just show a selection, changing it often enough to add variety and to help maintain a positive interest in the collection. If you pass by something every day, placed in exactly the same old spot, you will soon forget to look at it properly. But by going through the regular exercise of assessing which pieces to display for a time, deciding which objects look good arranged next to each other, and which to store for a period, you will learn more about your collection and it will always seem fresh. And every time you retrieve your favourite pieces from storage you will appreciate them anew, remembering what attracted you to them in the first place.

In a recessed window, John Rosselli has used the deep sill to create a formal grouping around an over-the-top English majolica urn made into a lamp, flanked by two pairs – one of majolica plates, the other of curious parakeets (above).

Green cabbageware, almost realistic enough to eat (right), is grouped on a wooden table with the addition of a vase of hydrangea flowers that tones, rather than contrasts, with the china. All is brought together by the colours of tapestry hung on the wall behind.

shape and form the elements are, the more tension and discipline there needs to be in their arrangement. It can never be just a question of putting everything down in one place. The placing must be as carefully thought out as the larger elements of the room.

Although it may seem like a contradiction in terms when displaying a collection, simplicity is essential. How to be simple when grouping things together is not easy, but it is vital. There must be space between each piece. Physical space, yes, but also a mental space – there is no room for unseen frills. This element may come through the background against which you show the collection. The background should be in contrast to the group, not a place into which objects melt and disappear, becoming indistinguishable from each other. Presentation is everything: many things benefit from a graphic approach. Small flat objects carefully collected, for example, can be framed individually or in groups of three or five, whether hung onto the wall or displayed on an easel. Be careful about symmetry, as it can all too easily degenerate into jarring rigidity. The eye requires balance, but it should be a balance of form and grouping; avoid having each object or element matching another with geometric precision.

As antique kitchenalia becomes a new area for collectors, an arrangement in the kitchen of a Normandy farmhouse, with each piece outlined against a white wall, shows how satisfying collecting together such simple shapes can be (right).

Even the simplest and most practical of kitchen utensils can look forceful when grouped together (below). These tall French oil jugs look graceful and elegant lined up on a windowsill, their delicate charm echoed by the sheer linen curtain.

A collection of antique glazed stoneware has been massed onto narrow shelves in a corridor in the Long Island home of collectors of early Americana. Whereas each piece might be appreciated when seen on its own, viewed in such profusion, it is possible to appreciate the art and skill which went into the making of these once everyday pieces (above).

One of the most beautiful and rewarding types of collection is what might be called natural curiosities. Historically, they were amassed and admired for their form and oddity value, achieving a particular vogue in Victorian times with the 19th-century trend of exploration, and the discovery of new species of plants in remote corners of the globe that could be brought home and established. For a while this century natural forms fell from favour; but now as we re-evaluate our shrinking world, they are valued once again as the amazing sculptures they are. Beloved by decorators and designers for their unique shapes, and also appreciated for the way

they juxtapose with pieces designed by man, they may be as simple as the long fronds of delicate black coral French designer Frédéric Méchiche displays in the tall black-and-white 18th-century containers in his country sitting room; as unusual as the spiky dried blowfish skeletons laid out on Christopher Hodsoll's sideboard; or even as quirky as the neatly labelled dinosaur bones Robert Kime displays on his rather grown-up version of a nature table, alongside towering containers of leaves, branches and blossom. It is the contrast between the discipline of man-made things and nature's lack of geometric discipline which is striking.

A mix of startlingly different elements still forms a cohesive collection: polished shiny metal bowls with their attendant candleholder; an inflated spiky blowfish; and a sophisticated, smooth lidded urn (above left).

The same idea repeated as often as one likes always makes for the successful display of any collection. Differently sized bronze sporting figures from the 19th and 20th centuries put together on the window and floor immediately catch the eye (top).

Where one nesting box is fun three are infinitely more fun. In decorator Bunny Williams's Connecticut house, these three sit on a table inside a covered porch – an invitation for broody birds (above).

A rural idyll in Normandy: on her desk, Annie Kuentzman-Levet puts together her collection of decoy ducks (anchored in upside-down flower pots) with a book of pressed flowers and plants as well as other pieces from a grown-up nature table (below).

Antique heart boxes, both American and English, laid out on a 17th-century Massachusetts table are so simple, and full of real charm. The lamp gives necessary height for the group (below top right).

Black on black – a collection of dark metal grouped, surprisingly, on the dark black of an antique range. All this would be too much were it not for the bright white wall behind (bottom right).

Incidentally, although flowers might not strictly be the remit of this book, flowers, leaves and potted plants are an important part of interior decoration, used both for themselves and as an integral part of a scheme or group. It might be stretching a point slightly to say flowers bring together a room, but they can add life where there is none. We are so used to seeing flowers in the house, but they were not much used thus until the 19th century – as revealed by 18th-century conversation piece paintings.

Today, flowers can often be used in a room in the same way that objects can to add scale and proportion and to lighten or alter an area –

again as with other objects the idea should be to use them in proportion. The most successful flower arrangements to use when combining pieces of different periods and places seem to be those which are relatively natural – urns full of flowering branches or tall flowering pot plants. Another way to show flowers to best effect – and to put to practical use some elements of certain collections as well – is to put separate bunches, each of a different kind of flower, in a group of similar china, silver or glass containers – perhaps yellow or blue and white. They should then be displayed quite closely together, or in small groups – three on a mantelpiece,

four on a long table. Or alternatively, take one particular sort of flower and show them in four or five very different bowls or jugs. The statement will be strong and different. The more formal the container, the more rural or informal the arrangement can often be. Silver or crystal glass jugs and urns, for example, whether or not they were actually designed for the purpose, look even better with flowers in them.

A collection can also be practical rather than purely decorative – something as mundane and as familiar as wooden breadboards, even in different sizes and shapes, look better ranged as a group against a wall or on a shelf, rather than hidden away in a cupboard. Other collections that perhaps had their origins in practical necessity consist of tools or sports equipment. Old specialist craftsmen's tools, such as blacksmith's tools or the wooden lasts used for shoemaking, are particularly prized

A collection is well displayed when there is a connection between the stage on which the collection stands, and the background or set which surrounds it. Harmony is achieved when the items in the collection somehow tie together the larger elements. This may be through colour – pulling one of the colours from the background into the foreground. Or

it may be through texture – repeating a particular texture both in the collection and in its background. Alternatively the colour of the backdrop can be in complete contrast to a collection. One particularly striking collection is simply a group of dark black-bronze figures and objects on the top of a matt black stove, the whole silhouetted against a white wall – this last giving the element of surprise and contrast.

Although a collection can be about things that are as small as toy cars, it can also be on a far wider scale – a concept in fact, or a theme, which runs through an entire house, influencing the choice of everything in it,

Even old metal watering cans can look special when grouped together in such a way that their elongated shape can be clearly seen (above). Sitting atop a tall cupboard and framed by the arch of the brick ceiling, the watering cans, with attendant birdcage also in metal, look about to soar away.

Simplicity itself is in this best of East and West detail. A carved wooden Eastern chair in front of an unadorned fireplace in London has, as the only decoration, a group of horn beakers ranged along the mantelpiece (below).

from furniture to fabrics to wall colour. The rooms becomes not merely the backgrounds for the objects, but also part of the same overall theme. It takes confidence and assurance to go this far, but when it is tastefully and successfully done, it is incredible.

However you put it together and whatever it consists of, a collection should make a harmonious group – a sight that is pleasing to the eye, both yours and that of others. A collection put together in this way allows the viewer to see a group of sometimes disparate objects in a new and defined light: each piece being an important part of the whole.

In this house in Tuscany, an interesting group is based on a collection of seven lidded glazed urns (opposite). Rather than just leave them on their own, they have been enhanced by the addition of some surreal metal wellington boots as well as other pieces on the table which add height and interest.

A collection is as much about shape as about content. Colour and shape are used again in Tuscany to make a small but pleasing arrangement above a mantelpiece in a bedroom (above). Blue and white spheres and circles sit on the mantelpiece itself against a delphinium blue wall and within the fireplace.

outdoor ornaments

Ornament is as important a part of the modern garden as it ever was of gardens of the past. Over the last few years the idea of interior decoration has gradually broadened to encompass the idea of exterior decoration as well. We have become more and more interested in the garden as an extension of the house and the pleasurable leisure activities that can take place there. It is no longer merely a place in which to cultivate flowers and vegetables, but an outdoor room.

Using ornament successfully outside the house depends very much on the near surroundings – whether horticultural or architectural. This commanding antique torso (above) stands in a small glade at the end of a leafy tunnel. Placing him here gives an emphasis and a point to both this walkway and others approaching it.

A gigantic ammonite sits inside a verdant conservatory (left). Surrounded by foliage, it looks as if it has just been unearthed.

As with so much in interior decoration, decorating the garden – and using ornament – is scarcely a new idea. From what still exists of Ancient Roman gardens we see how important the judicious use of ornament was – in buildings and statues, vases and urns, busts and masks. The Italian Renaissance brought the art of garden ornament to a peak – for at least 200 years no garden was complete without ornament used to mark a view or to prompt a moment of philosophical reflection.

Ornament, whether new or old, elevates a garden from the everyday to the sublime. Just as inside the house the right furniture and objects highlight the basic interior design as well as the architectural space, in the garden the right ornament acts as a counterpoint to the horticultural design, stressing what needs to be stressed, and defining what needs to be defined. Using various and varying kinds of ornament through the

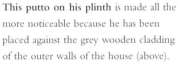

This putto on his plinth is made all the more noticeable because he has been placed against the grey wooden cladding of the outer walls of the house (above).

Happy the lion who sits outside in the sun and long grass all day enjoying the air, as this seemingly haphazardly placed stone lion (above right) is able to do.

Antique stone busts on plinths guard the entrance to a conservatory (right), acting also to define the heavy stone arched entrance to the delights beyond.

As important as it is inside the house is the careful grouping of shapes when working with ornament in the garden. Here, the large decorative pots are brought into focus with the addition of the angular stone pyramid in the foreground (above).

An ornate urn stands on an even more ornate plinth (above). The stately lines are softened by a profusion of informal planting: the urn itself is filled to overflowing with plants and the plinth is nestled among creeping groundcover and a rambling bush.

garden, whether it is a major construction such as a wooden pagoda or summerhouse or simply a stone urn, creates the sort of harmonious composition that is effective inside the house.

As in the house also, garden ornament today need not be old and need not be new. It can be either/or, and it can be a combination; equally the design of the garden itself can be classical or more contemporary in feel. Urns and urn-type vases are still the most popular type of free-standing garden ornament, used as they are for architectural balance as well as decoration and as containers. During the 18th century, garden urns were rarely used to hold flowers, but by the 19th century they were usually planted – several times during the year – with seasonal displays of flowers and plants, and they have become part of the horticultural scheme as well as the architectural one.

The garden is a fine example of a place where vastly different cultures and periods can be mixed with impunity. Large Eastern pots and drums can sit happily beside 18th-century stone pieces, 19th-century Victorian benches and 20th-century wire works. The universal green backdrop encompasses all.

Bunny Williams uses her Connecticut conservatory as a summer dining room and has furnished it accordingly, using garden ornament in a decorative manner (above). Here, an oversized urn is surrounded by plants and set in front of a dimly glassed mirror.

A stone trough planted with succulents adds an element of architecture (above left).

A blue-and-white urn with vibrant decoration is set among other pots and plants (left).

Sometimes the shape of a particular garden ornament is so pure that it needs almost nothing else. Here a tall glazed terracotta jar stands alone on a lawn in front of a low-branched orchard tree, each complementing the shape of the other (above).

Large sturdy clay pots are ideal for such ornamental flowers as lilies; their solid outline and unfussy lines anchor the showy flower spires admirably (above). Set either side of a garden door they are beautiful, and add gravitas to the garden.

Too often garden urns are planted with six bulbs or a row of sparse bedding plants. These two antique urns show how such containers – particularly if they are old – should be used for best effect (above right and right). Treated more like vases than planters, they exuberantly display flowers and foliage in a manner which would not look out of place inside the house.

But as with the inside of the house, care must be taken not to have too much of anything, and reference must always be made to the size of the garden when deciding on how to adorn it. In a small garden one single ornament can have as much impact as ten ornaments would in a larger garden, and vice versa. The eye is drawn toward any sort of ornamentation and it is vital that it seems appropriate and is in the right place. No ornament should be simply, as it were, dumped. It should be as carefully placed as a throne in a throne room, so that its impact and its help to the vistas of the garden are enhanced. This does not mean to say that it must always have a formal site cleared and arranged for it. It could, in the right garden and the right setting, just sit or even lie in long grass, be obscured by the lines of a tree, or be seen faintly in the dark edge of a leafy corner.

Garden furniture can also be considered to be part of garden ornament – although whether the ubiquitous white plastic moulded chair could be considered by anyone as decorative is debatable. But many furniture shapes – of chairs in particular, both very modern and quite antique – are fine in line and beautiful to

behold. Rustic chairs, especially those wooden ones created from twigs and branches of trees that look as though they will sprout leaves and start growing again at any moment, can look wonderful in a minimalist or paved garden. Iron work furniture was produced on a large scale in the 19th century, and many designs had sinuous iron leaves and flowers creeping through the ornate twisted iron branches. In fact, old metal furniture – tables, chairs and benches – of any design is decorative in the extreme and it does not even always have to be renovated. Other chairs to look out for are ones in cane or basket work or those once seen so often on American porches – comforting flat plank chairs with high backs and wide arm rests. Or use versions of the all-American rocking chair – so redolent of relaxing days in the summer sun.

The main thing, when using large-scale statuary, pieces of marble, stone and other objects designed originally to be seen outside, is not to be nervous of their scale. Use them on their own, mixed with other pieces in the same or similar materials, but use them boldly. In this garden conservatory (opposite), an assortment of old and beautiful objects in stone and marble welcome you inside.

An interesting and original use for a larger-than-lifesize warrior is in the entrance porch to a house, set against an old mirror which reflects mysteriously (left). Again, it is all a question of scale.

In New Jersey, John Rosselli combines different American pieces from different periods on his porch to make an eccentric-authentic American setting (below).

The height of a graceful female figure is combined with a terracotta pot on a marble-topped plinth (bottom). Once again scale is employed to good effect.

pictures and frames

It is now widely recognized that where pictures are concerned, the frame is as important as its contents – particularly when the frame is original to the picture. There are, today, so many pictures in galleries whose original frames were jettisoned by fashion diktats of the time and are lost forever; Napoleon was particularly guilty in this respect, ordering as he did the replacement of many of the frames of paintings in the Louvre, replacing them with frames designed in the latest style – Empire, naturally.

The frame of a picture should always be appropriate, both in design and in weight, to the picture it contains. There should be some intentional connection between the two, and the strength of subject must be matched by strength of mount and frame. Sometimes there is no need for a frame at all – many people prefer to let the picture speak for itself.

A picture in its frame is as much of an object as anything else in the room. It will be noticed as much and its positioning within the right scale and in proportion to everything else is just as important as any other group of objects. A Dutch painting in a heavy black frame in Lars Bolander's West Palm Beach house (above right) needs something definite beneath to anchor it to the floor. The small sofa and heavy carved wood double bowl suit the purpose and keep the group down to earth.

Off-white wooden walls act as a perfect foil both in colour and texture for any number of paintings. Here, a group has been made of both large and small pictures (right). Over the fireplace hangs the most dominant, with an almost equally large portrait of a man over a side table. To connect these, smaller pictures hang vertically between the larger ones.

Small pictures are hung to advantage against forgiving grey wooden walls (below): an ornate frame displays a medal; a frameless *trompe l'oeil* shelf makes the viewer look again; a grisaille trophy in the 18th-century manner depicts, instead of war, the more peaceful art of gardening.

Frames on their own can have a charm without the necessity of a picture (right). A frame in American decorator Laura Bohn's house has been laboriously decorated with small buttons and now is the centre of an eclectic group which includes old sepia photographs and a bleached white animal's skull.

A classic example of how to group small pictures to give them importance (bottom left): each is made part of a larger group with the oval of the mirror drawing the eye inwards. A chair placed precisely beneath the centre grounds the group.

A collection of seals set into an important frame is surrounded and framed again by a further collection of horns (below). Nothing else is needed.

When hanging pictures in any room, think of the overall graphic effect rather than just the personal quality of each picture. If your pictures are very good – museum quality even – then they should either hang alone or in a classically inspired group; if, on the other hand they are variable (like most people's) think of the overall effect, particularly in relation to the furniture within the room, something which many people do not do.

There is a conventional view of where on the walls pictures should be hung, but there is in fact no correct position. For example, in certain situations, pictures should be hung much lower than you would think – when the furniture is powerful, a low position gives pictures a strength that they would otherwise lose. Small pictures should not be hung in isolation, unless the space they fill is equally small; it would be preferable to hang them with more of the same, particularly if they have a medium or a theme in common – perhaps silhouettes, miniatures or pastels.

The relationship of background colour and picture colour ought to be considered. If a room is dark in tone or colour, hang the darker of your pictures there – glaringly pale pictures hung on dark walls in a room with little light offend the eye and the pictures jar. The same effect in reverse applies in light rooms: strongly coloured pictures will jump out from a weak background. There, hang your pale images – watercolours, drawings and so on. (If the room is too bright remember that you will need to have blinds or some other way of protecting the watercolours from the sun.)

It is important to think of a wider landscape than just a wall; pictures can and should be hung and displayed over a much wider variety of surfaces. They can sit on easels on tables (small pictures only) or propped in a line on the floor against the wall – a device which always makes people look twice – or against the wall, but perhaps at shelf or table height. They can be hung or propped on book shelves – both partially behind and in front of books. And they can be hung on screens – with perhaps a different grouping either side of the screen. Wooden shutters – those which fold into a deep reveal either side of the window – are another place to hang smaller pictures: hidden during the day, an unexpected scheme is revealed when the shutters are closed at night. Doors are another area too often ignored. The wooden panels can be too dominant in a room, but become part of it when broken up with pictures which fit inside each panel.

The way pictures are grouped is so important. A double column of classical prints runs all the way down one wall to skirting board level (far left). For good measure, another picture is also casually propped on the mantelpiece.

Frank Faulkner hangs his pictures with an artist's precision. Using furniture and objects as part of the group he executes a classical hanging (left). Three rondels he hangs vertically, repeating the shape with a circular glass on another wall (below).

Christopher Hodsoll combines old and new pictures and photographs on his staircase in an assured, casual manner (right). This group, united by their simple almost minimal frames, make a pleasing geometric design which is brought into focus by the small table and candlestick on the floor in front.

In this complex grouping not only are pictures propped on the shelves, but also figures and books (far right). Each piece has a precise part in the arrangement, which is pleasing and harmonious.

A potentially difficult to display collection of old photographs has been ranged along one end of the mantelpiece so that the varying frames, outlines and shapes of the pictures themselves become a group, regardless almost of their content (below). To the left, a large round mirror and an urn add depth, while to the right a screen bordered with a Greek key design adds a certain strength.

This complex satisfying arrangement (below) has been worked out from ground level up – from the rectangular baskets on the floor beneath the bench, to the pictures propped on books leading to the vertical line of pictures, and right across to the dark lamp leading into the large picture hanging above the table. As well as this carefully considered harmony of shape and form, there is also a colour tonality throughout the group.

There is no reason why pictures and photographs have to be hung at all; these black-and-white photographs are layered against an armoire and propped on the ground (above). This means that they can be easily re-arranged and re-appreciated according to whim.

This pseudo-rural grouping has been arranged in a most sophisticated manner (left). Centring on a collection of antique farm implements stacked in a large round wicker basket placed in the corner, the central group is surrounded by pictures of appropriate subject matter.

mirrors

Mirrors, or looking glasses, are important in every room, not only for checking one's reflection (although that is important), but because they add size as well as depth, and an air of mystery, opening unexpected vistas and reflections. When considering how best to use mirrors in a decorative scheme, it is instructive to look back to how they were used when rooms were lit in the evening only by candlelight. Think of Versailles, where the combination of flickering candles and the countless reflections conjured by so many mirrors hung together must have been magical.

Do not think of mirrors as pieces of glass within a frame hung on a wall – use them as decoration in their own right. Try resting a mirror against another, larger one, or propping a mirror against a fireplace. The frame is as important as the glass. It should be in proportion to the mirrored area; a looking glass of weight and importance should not have a narrow, mean frame. In fact, a mirror offers the opportunity to use a frame of the most ingenious design as there is no distraction from within its confines.

A concave mirror has been cleverly placed at the right angle of a staircase not only to reflect the picture arrangements, but also to give the pictures themselves greater importance (top).

An old glass is used not as a mirror but as an extra element: a way of highlighting and emphasizing the bust in front of it, and reflecting and extending the view of the room beyond (above).

Reality and surreality in Julie Prisca's Normandy house: a large zinc-framed mirror designed by her sits next to an empty painted-wood *trompe l'oeil* frame, also one of her designs (left).

A mirror is used as the centrepiece of a nautical group (left): the antique gilded frame sports dolphins below and a shell above and it is hung over a wooden model of a 19th-century sailing boat.

In this 18th-century panelled room in Paris, an area between the panelling has been fitted with sections of mirrored glass (left). In front of this a large Chinese painting has been hung in such a way that makes it almost appear to be floating.

A striped-seat chair sits underneath a very simple antique mirror which reflects the blue-white wall beyond (above).

An imposing convex mirror with gilded frame becomes the central feature of a group in a Swedish-inspired guest house in East Hampton (right).

Lighting

A jointed artist's figure has been made into a witty table lamp in a corner of Frank Faulkner's Manhattan loft (above). Ideally, table lamps in any room should always be viewed as part of the wider decorative group, rather than as solitary pieces of utilitarian equipment. This is an opportunity to create a group of interest and proportion (right).

The three absolutes of any decorative scheme are scale, proportion and lighting. The more diverse the room, the more crucial the lighting. It is no exaggeration to say that lighting, in the abstract, is the most important element in all interior decoration. The scheme can be perfect on paper – even perfect when you start to put it into place – but no matter how carefully you have thought it out and how painstakingly you have collected together all the right pieces, you will discover that all your little textural subtleties will be worth nothing unless they are properly lit.

In this formal and studied hall in London (right) the fine neoclassical table is made the centrepiece of this group, framed not only by candlesticks and candles which flank the wall mirror, but also by two wall lights set high to draw the eye up to the top of the composition.

In a beach guest cottage in East Hampton (far right) the simplicity of the walls of pale stained wood is matched by the naive, flower-headed girandole.

Unusually, artist Frank Faulkner uses flexible, angled desk lights as wall mounted lights in a corner of his Manhattan loft (below). They frame a formal composition which centres on one of his own paintings.

wall and ceiling lights

When creating an atmosphere in a room, lighting is, without doubt, the most important tool. If the lighting in a room is right, the other elements will fall into place with relative ease – or at any rate more so than if the lighting is completely wrong. Along with table and floor lamps, which are widely used, wall and ceiling lights can also have a place in certain rooms and situations – either as background lights which give an overall glow, or as attention-getters in their own right. While most of us have moved on from the single central ceiling light dangling unimaginatively from a flex, a central light fitting in chandelier or lantern form can be very effective when it is used in the right place, whether it is a genuine antique or a contemporary rendition of an old idea – over a dining table, for example, or in a bedroom or hallway.

Light fittings are an obvious way to mix styles and periods. Essential to the wellbeing of a room, lighting is now so technically advanced that old lights and decorative lights useful more for their aesthetic quality than their efficiency and practicality can be used freely against a controlled environment of dimmed and suffused background light. Ceiling and wall lighting can also be used as individual spotlights, look-at-me lights to throw some of the contents of a room into strong relief and to create hidden or exposed corners, even different moods, within the room.

Some of the most interesting contemporary design is in light fittings and fixtures, which is a very good thing, as an extremely modern light will often work amazingly well with an old piece of furniture or object. It is, as always, the contrast that pleases. Just as with single chairs, it is important to consider light fittings as objects, not merely as the tools of

Elaborate gilt and black wall sconces (left) hold candles which, rather than the customary white wax, are made from dark beeswax – an important detail.

A full-length painted trophy panel is framed by unusual French lanterns made from tin (above). A terracotta bust set high on a plinth balances the group.

function and necessity. A lamp which is an attractive entity in its own right, whether new or old, can be used not only to provide light, but also to punctuate and frame other objects and pieces of furniture, as artist Frank Faulkner has done so well in his New York loft.

While contemporary light fittings are valued for their challenging nonconformity and the diversity they can introduce into an arrangement that includes period pieces, traditionally designed light fittings also have their place in a mixed scheme. Chandeliers, in particular, are once again being appreciated as objects of often considerable beauty, and they can work as well in a modern interior as in one which is faithful to a period style. They were first depicted in 17th-century Dutch paintings, usually

A formal arrangement of seat, painting, table and screen (below) is spotlit by a discreet, modern inset ceiling light.

An antique chandelier, like this one in Robert Kime's drawing room (right), is a thing of beauty, whether it is used or not.

The fragile delicacy of this fine 18th-century chandelier in Paris (far right) is accentuated by the contrast with the 1940's furniture in the room below.

made of brass; and over the next hundred years, chandeliers developed into beautiful, elaborate confections of sparkling, glassy art. As they hung suspended from the ceiling, with their ropes and droplets of crystal or glass swagged round branches holding sometimes dozens of candles, they reflected and softened the light in an almost magical way. Usually hung much lower than they would be today, even allowing for the much higher ceilings of the time, they were a striking focal point in the room.

Over the last twenty or thirty years chandeliers have not been so much in favour – possibly due in part to the increased manufacture of various cheap imitations of the originals, in which a cursory design of roughly moulded glass droplets slung round coarse branches from which shone too many over-bright harsh electric candle-shaped bulbs which left no corner of a room unturned. But as with everything beautiful, chandeliers very much have a place today. An old crystal one – even if it has a few droplets missing – can add focus to a large drawing room; or perhaps a more modest example with coloured glass droplets would be appropriate in a bedroom covered with toile de Jouy designs; or even hung low, and used as originally designed, with candles, over a dining table. Antique chandeliers can, with some minor modifications, be electrified, but where it is possible to accommodate the restrictions of candlelight, it is better by far to remain true to the intended effect.

Lanterns too, like candelabra, are being seen in a new way. Made for many centuries in both the East and the West, they can be used – in original form and also as reproduction designs – both inside and outside the house. Moroccan and Turkish lanterns, for example, with their panes of coloured and decorated glass, look good not only in conservatories as seen here, but also as a solution for the perennial problem of an overhead light in a hall or corridor – indeed in any room where a ceiling light is essential, although not often used. With their enclosed design, lanterns look good even when viewed from above, say from an upper landing, so they are also useful on staircases. Out of doors, lanterns in metal or glass look just as good during the day as they do when illuminated at night.

Only a decorator confident of his own taste, as is Robert Kime, would hang a chandelier in a conservatory – where it looks unexpected and wonderful (far left).

Eastern lanterns, which often have coloured and decorated panes of glass, look particularly good in a conservatory, especially when different types are grouped together (left and below).

Wall-attached candle holders – sconces – are also enjoying a new and well-deserved popularity. Sconces can be antique, they can be traditional in design or they can be contemporary, ranging from ornate gilded brackets to naive country-style twisted wood – whatever style they are in, they can be used, as shown throughout this book, to add particular definition to a grouping or arrangement of furniture and objects, as well as being a useful additional source of light in a room.

Perhaps most versatile and useful of all where candlelight is needed or wanted is the branched candlestick – a candelabra. Holding two, four, or even six candles, candelabra are adaptable as well as attractive. They can be old and made of silver, metal, glass (sometimes with delicate baby chains of glass droplets) or even plasterwork; or they can be overtly modern in design. Either type will work well with other periods of furniture or objects, serving either to emphasize or contrast. In addition candelabra are invaluable for adding strong vertical structure to any arrangement. A mixed collection of single candelabra made in one material – say brass or glass – of differing heights and designs, can be used on a dining table to great effect. A word also about the colour of candles: although there are exceptions – the natural dull amber of a beeswax candle, say, or sometimes a dramatic black or gold – on the whole, candles – like bedlinen – look best in simple white or ivory.

lamps

Floor and table lamps are an integral part of any lighting scheme. As well as giving light, they can and should be used to give mass and volume to any decorative scheme. A natural focus when alight, a lamp adds valuable height and definition to a table group. In a large room, one which has places for many lamps, vary the shape as well as the age of the bases as much as possible – old and new, square and round, work much better than a deadening conformity.

While old lamps can be converted gas lanterns, they can also be made most successfully from things that were not originally designed to act in such a capacity. Obvious candidates for the make-over treatment can include bronzes, vases, urns, spelter or terracotta figures and glass jars.

With lamps, particularly old lamps made from sometimes ornate antique vases and pots, it is important to pay great attention to the shape and material of the shade. Many a beautiful old lamp base has been ruined by being paired with the wrong sort and size of shade. As always, it is best not to be too clever and to let the shape of the shade follow the line of the lamp, but not to match it exactly. Over the last few years, shades have decreased slightly in size in relation to the base of the lamp. An overblown tall drum or cylindrically shaped shade now looks out of balance somehow, and more subtle shapes are preferred. With table lamps, it is vital that they be put on a table of the right height – too high and they blind those who sit near them, too low and an unflattering spotlight is cast upwards.

Julie Prisca is multi-talented, designing not only the metal furniture seen here, but also the sinuous floor light, and the table lamp (opposite) which both work well with the antique pieces on the right.

On a console table of her own design, Julie Prisca arranges ultra-narrow metal lights which spotlight yet do not detract from the wall-hung plaster relief (above).

An eclectic arrangement that includes an empty frame against the wall and a Mies van der Rohe Barcelona chair is given precision by the table lamps (top right).

An antique canister made into a lamp is an integral and essential part of this decorative composition (centre right).

Although not of the same period, the urn lamp base and the small iron table are brought together by the Greek key-patterned screen (right).

Rooms

The arrangement of rooms was something into which architects put much thought: it was an essential part of their craft and expected by their clients. Rooms were arranged according to an understood set of rules – rules of proportion and scale, almost mathematical in concept, that were first used in architecture by the Ancient Greeks and Romans. Although the rooms we arrange today are different in detail from those of 200 years ago, the same rules apply. Every room must still be a complete composition, with a balance of harmony and scale and all that implies.

Applying such concepts to the arrangement of a room does not guarantee instant taste – that is altogether a more elusive skill – but it does allow for a certain harmony. Take the question of scale. This really means the distribution of masses and the knowledge that nothing in a room should overpower anything else. Towering cupboards should not be teamed with delicate, spindly-legged tables. Porcelain figurines 20 cm tall should not stand next to 15-cm high carved African masks. It is a question of proportion. When everything is in the right scale, the walls of the room recede and the room feels larger.

A room must also have balance. This should not be confused with symmetry and does not mean that everything should be matched, for therein lies monotony. Symmetry should be underneath the structure, in the bones of the room, not on the surface. Most decorators today will, in any room, break up sets (of lamps, tables, chairs) to avoid a look that carries the vestiges of the infamous enthusiasm for 'mix n' match'.

In a text book case of how to use texture to underline the beauty of specific objects, Frédéric Méchiche, to great effect, contrasts on two different walls in the same room an exquisite 18th-century porcelain group (above), and two ceramic ovals against, seemingly rough and distressed, but actually subtly coloured, plaster wall (above right).

Colour and Texture

Though less obviously visible at first sight than the furniture or furnishings, colour and texture are none the less vital elements of the well-arranged room. Colour not only sets the scene, it can also be used as balance or counterbalance to a piece of furniture or architectural feature. A block of strong colour can balance a heavy cupboard or desk in the same manner as a piece of furniture might. Colour can cohere, draw in, pull together. Colour can and should be used as a connector as well as a contrast, not just on walls or upholstery but by bringing together everything within that colour palette, so that styles and periods can be mixed with abandon.

Texture too is vital: not only the texture of different fabrics in soft furnishings but the interplay of rough with smooth – concrete against velvet, metal against wood. How these

In their bastide in Provence, Irene and artist Giorgio Silvagni use colour in their kitchen as an unifier: not only to display their Vallauris pottery against a wall of warm terracotta (below left), but also to hang a console made from an old iron balcony and a sconce made from a piece of 16th-century carved wood (right).

textures are used is the key. The texture of a wall can be used as a foil for the things within the immediate area; the texture of furnishings as an element of comfort within the whole room.

Colour on the walls is all important – it can be used to bring an air of mystery and romance to a space. It is the background against which all else is judged and of which all must become part. A good wall colour can go a long way toward making less interesting pieces appear rather more interesting. In general a 'good' wall colour is one that is warm and inviting, not overpowering, subtle and yet not boring – one which pleases the eye without assaulting it. Without a background there can be no foreground, and colour provides that background. When used decisively, it can successfully marry two periods, particularly if the dominant background colour is a soft glazed tone – a shade that just might conceivably have come from another time. Many decorators now specialize in creating colours like this – perhaps of today, possibly from yesterday, maybe of tomorrow.

Some very confident spirits take the idea of borrowing colour from the past even further and incorporate texture, too, by distressing the walls in an inventive, original way, working some colour in, rubbing colour out, creating a background of layers, some strong, some subtle. To distress successfully needs great confidence and subtlety, otherwise it can just look as if the wall, and indeed the whole house, is about to fall down; or worse, you can produce a horrible hotchpotch of glaring hues. But done with artistic skill, it is a revelation.

Although distressed colour is obviously not for everyone, it is just one example of the sort of experimentation with colour that everyone should try. Colour changes constantly with the light, reflecting and altering the surfaces – not only of the walls but of everything within the room. These days you do not see many rooms painted in strong primary colours and finished with contrasting brilliant-white woodwork. This is all to the good; such contrasts did little for the room or its contents. Today, preferred tones as far as the woodwork and surrounds are concerned are either a softer tone of the wall colour or a muted white-ivory shade.

When thinking about what colour to use, do not think simply in terms of strong shades – neutrals are colours as well and can be used very successfully, particularly in a room where all the other elements are so disparate. Monochromes too, boldly used together with different textures and tones, can have just as colourful an impact as more obvious hues. Or take a tone from one

of the elements in the room – perhaps from a piece of china or a textile on a cushion – and repeat that tone in something much larger in scale, such as the upholstery of a chair or the colour of a wall.

Colour can also unify a group, regardless of whether it is large or small. Think of a group of jugs of different sizes or styles – if they are all yellow they become a coherent group not just a mixture of old bits of china; think also of a group of seating in a room – if all of the chairs are unified by just a streak of the same colour somewhere in each one then suddenly there is a coherency that would not otherwise exist.

Although colour can of course be bright it should never be allowed to overwhelm or overpower. It should not be used in obvious ways – many decorators, for example, feel that a dark room should be kept dark, not painted a bright or very pale colour – although conversely bright touches against the darker background will help bring the darker colour alive. Generally, rather than contrasting colours, whether light or dark, go for complementary ones. The effect is more subtle.

When deciding on a colour or colours for a room and thinking about whether it should be textured or not, bear in mind that as decorating techniques they are both affected by the geographical location of the room or house. The dark Renaissance colours so successfully used in hot climates can work in breezy northern rooms. but they should be subtler, and usually softer in tone. So it is with distressing. The undeniable charm of a heavily distressed wall could simply look, on a rainy, cold, northern day as if the room is in dire need of damp-proofing.

Irene and Giorgio Silvagni use colour in an emphatic way to accentuate everything in their house, particularly Irene's large collection of textiles, many of them old quilts and hangings (far left). Here, a day bed is covered in an antique quilt, and cushioned with different red and white textiles, all against a vibrant background of red distressed plaster walls, painted by Giorgio Silvagni.

Colour can transform a piece of furniture, the soft tones of the painting linking with both the chest and even the bowl upon it (above).

Even the most aesthetically perfect piece of furniture – in this case a cabinet that is neoclassical in design – can be taken into a different dimension with the right use of very bold colour (left).

Colour can be used in an ingenious way to tie different styles and periods together. Here, against hyacinth blue walls, small groups have been put together which have an impact going far beyond the different individual components (left and below). The only link between the various ornaments is colour – that, and a discipline of shape.

A dovecote converted into a bedroom (above) offers a natural display cabinet for objects against a wall of heavenly blue.

There is something about the soft yellow of this wall which brings everything together – leather, wood and even the fragile branch of coral (right).

The painted floor and softly coloured walls act as a subtle background for this strong mixed collection of dark, heavy objects (opposite).

Flooring

The decoration and finish of floors has always been important, for what happens at floor level is vital to the ultimate success of the completed room. Every good designer starts with the floor, deciding on what will in effect be the canvas for the finished look. However much artifice you apply, what is certain is that any floor treatment, no matter how simple, can change the look of the whole room immediately, for what is on the floor can unify and pull together in the most dramatic way imaginable.

In Frédéric Méchiche's Paris apartment the diamond-patterned stone floor of his hall sets the tone for the decorative scheme (below). An 18th-century bench – which was a working rather than a courtly piece – is painted and upholstered in a bold black-and-white stripe. Above hangs an even bolder contemporary painting, and in the window to the courtyard a sculpture balances the weight of the painting.

A well-proportioned inner hall with corresponding floor space in Christopher Gibbs's Oxfordshire home requires several rugs – all toning with each other to fill the area satisfactorily (right).

Architects and builders thought about flooring remarkably early on – the Romans made terracotta tiles in Britain and of course laid those complex mosaic floors, remnants of which can still be seen. Later, popular choices were wood, local stone or marble. By the 17th century some houses had noteworthy floors with – in the principal ground-floor rooms – lead-glazed tiles and black-and-white marble tiles, while rooms above ground level were finished with boards.

Surprisingly, many old floors have remained relatively intact, and should you be so lucky as to have an original floor, you can do no better than to restore it as well as possible, nourish it, preserve it and flaunt it. If the floor is of stone or tiles in relatively good condition, they may be cleaned and sealed. The floor may be made from plain wooden boards; although these may have not been polished originally (unadorned wooden floors were most often cleaned with damp sand and then dry-rubbed) today people seem to prefer to see a glow to wooden boards – though preferably not the unnatural high shine achieved by using gloss varnish. Whether old or new, board floors may be, according to their condition, colour-stained or painted and waxed in a single colour, as well as sealed and polished in their natural state. The choice of stains and paints which can be used on the floor

In this Swedish-style guest house in East Hampton, the floor is painted with a seemingly simple but actually intricate design against a sea-colour stained wall (left).

On the cobbled floor of Irene and Giorgio's Silvagni's living room – it used to be the courtyard – an oversized smooth-sided terracotta pot tones with the wall and balances the roughness of the cobbles (right).

A faded but beautiful early tapestry carpet has its subtle tones emphasized by the stained floorboards, the colour of which has been chosen to bring out the subtle tones of the rug (below).

is far wider today than ever before, and colours can be combined for really interesting results.

Wooden floors can also be decorated with a pattern, painted freehand or stencilled. Designs are based on many sources, from European folk art to classical designs and can be basic two-colour combinations, or multi-coloured designs in varying degrees of sophistication. Painted floors were a traditional form of decoration where costly rugs could not be used. In America especially, during the early years of the colonies, the painting of floors became elevated to an art form – with designs either stencilled or just painted in geometric designs and clear colours.

But many old floors today are badly worn, damaged or uninspiring, and the designer may decide to completely cover the existing floor with something as simple as sea grass, sisal or flat weave carpet in order to give an even, neutral surface on which he or she can add and build in terms of brighter rugs and other carpets. So strong colour here is to be avoided. A neutral grey-ish beige is usually the answer – the colour the British decorator John Fowler (1906–77) christened 'mouseback'.

Once the base ground is decided on, the contrast, if any, should be considered. If the floor is painted – particularly in what might be described as a painterly manner – it may not be

Although fitted all-over patterned carpets were recorded nearly 200 years ago, the ubiquitous plain fitted carpet has not been with us nearly so long. Its popularity was to the detriment of loose rugs, and for some years the floors of thousands of houses were covered in wall-to-wall carpet – boring but supposedly safe.

Central heating and a renewed pleasure in natural finishes have both led to a resurgence in the popularity of floorboards, but if you have inherited a fitted carpet, and you do not wish to remove it, whether for practical or aesthetic reasons, then use the fitted carpet as the most basic of backgrounds, and place several rugs over it – and even over each other, particularly if the rugs are old and woven with vegetable-dyed fibres. Do not try to look for rugs that match – it is much better that they should not. The only thing you need to take into account is the type of pattern – different geometric designs work well together, or different floral

necessary, or advisable, to put anything else on it, particularly in a warm climate. But if you do, then the obvious addition would be a rug.

Since they were first woven (which they have been for at least 700 years, and probably longer) carpets and rugs have long been prized in Europe. Paintings from as early as the 15th century show that these valued possessions were not put on the floor. Mats of rush or straw were used there instead, while the precious carpets were used either as hangings or were draped over tables rather than on the floor where they might have been damaged. By the middle of the 18th century, carpets, in large houses at any rate, were quite usual, either imported from the East or made in England – carpets were now being made at Axminster, Wilton and Kidderminster. Robert Adam's designs in grand houses such as Syon and Osterley showed the carpet in an even more prominent light, and from then on they were a desirable element in all the best houses.

If the floorboards are good enough and the staircase above it rises with dignity, just leave well alone, without colour or treatments, as Frédéric Méchiche has done in his Paris apartment (above).

In Frédéric Méchiche's house near Toulon, the rough bricks of the staircase are accentuated by the distressed colour of the walls (right).

Christopher Hodsoll uses a patterned stair runner on his staircase, which is accentuated by white painted surrounds and pictures displayed in seemingly casual manner on every tread (below).

patterns, but usually not both together, unless of course they are linked by colour.

Proportion and scale are again important. If you have a small rug, do not leave it marooned. Either anchor it with several others or put it in a corner or part of the room where it becomes part of a scheme. Nothing looks lonelier than a huge acre of plain carpet or wood or stone floor with a single small rug in front of the fire or in the centre. Better not to have one at all.

Traditionally carpet or rug was laid on polished boards, but a contrast of texture between floor and rug is far more appealing. Flat woven or embroidered stitched rugs look wonderful on a shiny surface – wood or stone. Rough boards underneath an Aubusson or on a painted floor surprise the eye and give a new interest to the surface. Painted floors in patterns reminiscent of Dutch or German designs need no covering, and a sophisticated carpet often looks better on

a fairly rough planked floor which has been lightly stained or painted, than on parquet or marquetry. Again it is the contrast – light against dark, rough against smooth, that works.

A hand-sewn tapestry rug by artist Phoebe Hart of a favourite dog looks well against a rug of a paler hue in this East Hampton beach house (left).

Sophisticated simplicity: not only is the floor painted in tone-on-tone diamonds, but the staircase is Scandinavian blue with contrasting terracotta treads (below).

Living Rooms

Living rooms can come in many guises; they can be anything that you care to make them. And what you do make of them is very important indeed. First impressions are important, and for many of your guests the living room will be the first, and very often the only, room that they will see. So think long and hard before you make decisions.

The Tuscan living room of architect Piero Castellini Baldissera (left and above) is both comfortable and sophisticated. The varied and catholic group of objects and furniture are firmly welded together by strong, cool colours and textures.

The history of domestic architecture and design is largely the history of the development of privacy and comfort. For several centuries comfort was neither a priority nor even a desirability, and privacy was not even an issue. But as domestic life became ever more sophisticated, the need for a wider range of private quarters became apparent, and over the centuries new, more compact rooms were added to the original communal areas, which were still used as places of reception, dining and business.

By the 17th century, among these new, more intimate spaces, the withdrawing room eventually evolved, a room which itself developed from the gallery – the long upper-storeyed, windowed room where works of art were displayed and exercise taken in inclement weather. This new withdrawing room was at first a place to which ladies could retire, away from the raucous pleasures of the male-dominated dining room. But by the 18th century the drawing room had become a room in its own right – no longer merely as a withdrawing room with the attendant sitting and waiting the name somehow implies, but rather as a room of pastimes, pleasure and above all, comfortable living. It was always a room which retained an essentially feminine aspect, as opposed to the more predominantly masculine feel of the dining room and study.

Whether it is in his sophisticated Paris flat (below, right and opposite below) or his far simpler country house near Toulon (opposite above), Frédéric Méchiche combines furniture and objects in a truly original way. In Paris, he combines 18th-century furniture, unvaryingly covered in cream or white natural fabric, and much of it painted, with sculpture and pieces from every century and continent. The colour palette, even of the many paintings and artworks, is kept strictly monochrome, which successfully creates an overwhelmingly contemporary feel.

Today, although its purpose appears clear, in fact everyone views the drawing room (living room, sitting room – whatever you prefer to call it) in a different way. In a large house there may be both a drawing room and a sitting room, the first a room of formal entertainment, the second a

room of everyday use. In most houses, however, there is just one general living room and how that is decorated depends greatly on the priorities within the family or group. It is, after all, either a room with no specific use or a room with every conceivable use, and these conflicting definitions

The refined lines of a Louis XVI mirror, a Directoire chair and English Regency candlesticks are emphasized by the collection of bleached-out coral and exotic shells in Méchiche's sunny southern France living room (above).

In a corner of his Paris drawing room (below), Méchiche places a low chair by the 18th-century master chair maker Georges Jacob in juxtaposition to an exuberant 20th-century sculpture by Nikki de St Phalle on a white plinth.

In Normandy, Annie Kuentzman-Levet has designed the living area to not only combine different functions, but also to be warm and cosy (below).

Different periods, styles and colours are combined to create a room that is completely unified in purpose (right).

In this small sitting room in Alidad's London home there are over twenty different patterns – on walls, ceiling, floor and furnishings – and it is a testament to his skill that the finished effect is harmonious and comfortable (opposite).

mean that it is difficult to decorate a room in such a way that it has both an identity and a feeling of comfort and of practicality. Perhaps that is why many living rooms look ugly or, more often, boring and uncomfortable. Torn between the disparate needs and priorities of different people and different activities, the room ends up with no clear identity of any sort.

The first thing to ascertain before getting on to the refinements of the decoration is to question how the room will be used over the course of each day. For entertainment? Entertainment plus relaxation? Plus work or study? And eating also? And will it be used throughout the day, or only in the evening? Poor old living room – no wonder it can look such a mess.

While thinking about the functions of your particular room, bear in mind that throughout everything a living room should first and foremost be just that – a place where domestic life can be lived with ease and in comfort as well as somewhere where friends can be entertained. It should reflect leisure and a general enjoyment of life; the best rooms, wherever they are, have a certain unpretentiousness and ease of manner.

Once you are clear on what role – or roles – you require the room to fulfil, then you can think about how arrange it. When considering how to design and decorate a particular room, all good designers and decorators start first with the basic architecture of the building, for although they are working on the interior rather than the exterior, the latter influences the design of the former. The best interior design is always harmonious with, and appropriate to, the architecture of the house.

From the first house dwellers on, it was understood that a house has a spirit and it is important to respect that spirit. Simply, this means that successful decoration and successful combinations of furniture come from using things, ideas and colours that fit in with the house, with its style and its proportions and scale. This does not mean everything should be the same, and everything fit in with everything else; rather it means all should be in sympathy with each other. It is about fusing styles and shapes. What it must not be is an uncoordinated aimless mixing of everything into a discordant chaos. When combining styles and periods, no one style or period should dominate or overpower. Architecture is about proportion and scale, and so is design. Almost always when people say that a room is 'just not quite right, although I can't put my finger on exactly why,' it is nearly always a question of wrong proportion.

In classical architecture, and later during the 18th- to 19th-century neo-classical revival, the proportions of the room were calculated with almost mathematical precision, and rigidly applied. The ratio of skirting to dado, dado to wall, and wall to picture rail and cornice were absolutes not to be departed from – and the results were pleasing and harmonious. So when arranging the room – particularly when using all those different pieces from different places, the standard rules apply even more strongly.

First, let's consider scale. When anyone mentions scale, what they really mean is scaling up – not scaling down. Small pieces in a small room do not work in the way one might think they would; conversely, large pieces in a small room can make it seem both larger and more comfortable. If among your chosen bits of furniture there are pieces which vary wildly in scale the smaller pieces must be made to balance the larger. This means that small pieces must not be left to stand alone, but must be massed – either with colour or texture, or made part of a group: a small table, for example, might be flanked by two chairs, and have a picture or pictures hung above it so that the eye is taken upward and outward, and the table is perceived as larger than it actually is.

Continuity of line and scale is important when mixing differing styles of furniture together in a living room. With chairs, for example, a round-backed contemporary chair will look perfectly at ease with a similarly shaped antique chair, as long as they are both of a relatively similar height. Conversely, a contrast of shape can often also work, each piece throwing the other into relief. But if you do decide to go this route, it is even more important that the scale – the relative height and width of each chair – be sympathetic. Disparately styled chairs grouped in front of a screen, wall hanging or curtain – something with a certain fluidity – will be also pulled together by this type of background.

Once these early decisions have been made, the next stage is to decide precisely what pieces of furniture will be necessary. Start, as always, with the minimum and build up from there. Too often the living room is used as the place to deposit all that furniture for which no one can find a home elsewhere. There may be a sofa donated from someone else's house ('too good to throw away', they try to persuade you) a new, particularly comfortable chair, a junk shop must-have, and some large old piece that was inherited – perhaps a bookcase, a bureau or a tall cupboard. Sadly, with the best will in the world, what you cannot do is simply mix everything together in a wonderful jumble and hope against hope that it will all, in some miraculous way, come together, for it will not. Intelligent selection is the key to getting the space right, combined with some imagination and, it has to be said, a bit of confidence – which of course you will have acquired after reading this book.

Lars Bolander's eclectic grouping in his West Palm Beach living room warrants detailed examination (far left) Different periods and cultures are all brought together with harmonious results.

John Rosselli's summer sitting room in New Jersey – a converted barn – is boldly furnished (left and below). The dramatic beamed ceiling and wide open-plan space makes it possible for him to use large-scale pieces of furniture and objects and to combine them with American brio.

These factors notwithstanding, however, to combine disparate shapes and styles does require some discipline and thought, and it is important to remember that furniture is not just a series of pieces, each with its own function – a sofa, a chair, a low table. Designers and decorators will tell you that in every room each piece, every object, should be looked at carefully for what it is in itself – in the same way you would look at a hat or a handbag – to see what aesthetic, or unique quality, each piece has. Then, and only then, can all the pieces be looked at together to see how the whole effect can add to the overall harmony of the room, and where each piece will look and function best.

Photographing the homes of designers all over the world you realize that they never take anything for granted. Everything – down to the smallest shelf – is observed minutely, considered and appreciated. Only then is it thought about in the context of a particular room. One realizes how often we only really half look at a piece of furniture – 'nice chair', 'good table' – while not actually taking into account what the piece can do for both us and the room. The message is that nothing that you like is useless. It may not go in that particular room, but it will go somewhere, and it is surprising what will work under an expert's eye. In interior designer Lars Bolander's sitting room in West Palm Beach, for

Two different views of Robert Kime's comfortable and welcoming Wiltshire drawing room (top left and centre) demonstrate the seemingly effortless ease with which he combines objects and textiles, each piece of the whole – from the grand chandelier to the charmingly sprawling flower arrangement – of the right scale and in proportion to everything else.

Alidad's London drawing room combines colour and pattern, texture and textile (top right). One of the reasons the scheme works so successfully is because of the conscious lack of symmetry in the arrangement. In contrast, this living room designed by Prue Lane (above) applauds the occasional merits of symmetry as a device to bind two different cultures – East and West – together.

In **John Rosselli's** New Jersey drawing room, large scale pieces of furniture are balanced by using a collection of blue-and-white ceramics on the far wall (far left).

Frank Faulkner has created a distinctive living area in his large Manhattan loft by arranging together an eclectic selection of comfortable chairs surrounded by tables of an appropriate height (left).

Shapes and periods – a 19th-century iron day bed and a modern upholstered stool – are combined to make a room both neoclassical and contemporary (below).

A **charming summer** guest house on Long Island is comfortably furnished in holiday mood (above). The painted floor and decorated ceiling beams anchor a scheme that includes painted Swedish furniture, Indian fabrics and an antique fireplace, combined with modern accessories.

example, there is a mix of so many unusual things – an Indian bed used as a table, a French metal stool, a leopard-skin covered sofa, Indian fabric and 19th-century reproduction pictures – and they combine together wonderfully. All

the pieces do have a certain sophistication and on the whole sophisticated, what one might call 'town' furniture, does not go hand in hand with simpler, naive 'country' furniture. (Although, in the same way that a basic dress can be thrown

into focus by being worn with a witty hat or an eccentric pair of shoes, a simple scheme can be highlighted by the addition of a strangely shaped chair or an unusual cushion. It is not easy, but thought and an aware eye will work miracles.)

Looking at the living rooms illustrated on these pages, it is evident that all but the tiniest have, whether deliberately or not, been divided into two or more smaller, distinct spaces. Any room needs at least one point of interest, and in a

Another light-filled room on Long Island has a blue-painted wooden and cane sofa with a thick padded seat that has been covered with mattress ticking and cushioned with layers of old French quilts (above). The judicious use of colour ties this room together.

larger or unconventionally shaped room at least two, possibly more. There may be a convivial conversation space, grouped around a fireplace; and a reading area, well lit, with comfortable chairs and books to hand; and perhaps a writing space with desk or table and one or two chairs. There may even be, in the hardest working of these rooms, a dining area with a table and yet another grouping of chairs. Comfort in a living room – in any room – is all important. These are houses, not museum exhibits. Lars Bolander, Christophe Gollut and Robert Kime are just a few of the too-many-to-list decorators who do not like things that are too perfect or always come in pairs. So the way to avoid this dreadful solecism is, of course, to mix.

Within the different groupings of the perfect living room, different periods and styles can be mixed because they are drawn together by their shared function. Oddly, although this might sound complicated, it is in fact easier to think of a sitting room in these terms than simply as one vast living area. The rooms which do not work are those in which furniture and furnishings are adrift – placed simply to fill an empty space. Even a very large space like that of a loft can be made to look comfortable, interesting and even cosy when the furniture grouping is confident and broken up. And there should be access from each area to the other spots. Navigation around chairs or tables should not be necessary.

One of the most useful of devices when dividing a living area into different spaces is the ubiquitous screen. Once invaluable to ward off niggling little draughts in houses which were not heated, screens now have another role to play, and whether it is a lacquered Coromandel screen of great value and drama, or painted plywood panels held together with hinges, nothing defines like a screen. Not only does it mark off one space from another but, because of its panel construction, it is a doubly effective decorating device, as it can be used behind a group of, let's

In a sky-lit Paris flat designed by architect Olivier Vidal, one quite narrow but long space functions as a complete living area, and combines several very strong pieces of furniture – all very different periods and styles (left and above). However, the skilful arrangement of the room means that everything works together really well.

say, chairs, and will enclose and encompass them, making them into a cohesive group, suddenly linking each piece with its neighbour. This can be particularly useful when the objects are of different shapes or periods. If a screen is highly decorated what you place in front of it should be simple in form and not over-ornamented. If, however, the screen is textured – covered with a plain material or simply made of wood – then the pieces it frames can be of intricate variety. It can also be used, if it is fairly plain and uniform, as a background on which to hang pictures, or stand a sculpture against, thus forming what is in effect a new living and display area.

In any room that must serve a number of different purposes nothing can be planned in isolation, and the more varied the options the better will be the result. Try the unusual thing, the unpredictable. It gives a room an edge and a sense of excitement. A surprise always adds interest. It can be small – such as a striking cushion or an unexpected bowl – but a good room does surprise, and does interest, and that makes people use it even more.

Dining Rooms

More than any other room in the house, the dining room is where different periods, styles, even tastes, can be put together with confidence. A dining room is one of the few places in the house where people are – for a time – sitting in one place and where therefore the eye can be drawn towards dramatic objects and groupings around the room.

In artist Frank Faulkner's loft the dining area brings together disparate styles and periods, all of which he has combined with skill. Against a screen displaying pictures painted by the artist is a long French cheese table (above). This in turn anchors the new fibreboard and metal dining table (left). The objects – a wooden column, metal candlesticks, a terracotta Chinese horse on a lacquered box, and, on either side, a pair of shallow tazze on more wooden columns – give order and proportion to a group of very different elements.

When you think about it, the dining room in all its frosty splendour has been with us for a remarkably short space of time. In medieval times, public meals were taken originally in the great hall – effectively the only general reception room – and then later in the great chamber. Although by the 17th century some European houses boasted a room with a large immoveable eating table, in most houses at that time meals were taken in a variety of different rooms, anywhere, in fact, that seemed like the right place at that particular moment – this room for the light, this for the heat. People ate from folding tables that were put up where needed.

Gradually, by the middle of the 18th century, one particular and more intimate room became designated solely for the eating of meals. This room contained a single table, often with extending leaves, and which was far lighter in appearance – in shape and in finish – than the heavy old oak refectory tables. It was about this time that the dining room came to be considered as a room of some importance and status, a room for the receiving of guests, indeed – a fact still acknowledged by its nomenclature as a 'reception room' in estate agents' particulars. Architects like Robert Adam and William Kent designed dining tables with chairs that stood against the wall and were pulled forward when required. There were also buffets, or sideboards, huge urn or coffer-shaped wine coolers, and other imposing pieces made in gilded and ornamented mahogany and other fine woods. Silver- and goldsmiths produced ornate, fantastic centrepieces for the table, designed to represent everything from dolphins and castles to serpentine flora and fauna. It would probably be true to say that not

The confident lines of the period furniture in this neoclassical dining room (above) are made more of by the startling pink wall colour and the contemporary abstract painting.

Christophe Gollut's deceptive study/dining room seems to be a period piece (left and right), but it conceals all the components of an efficient kitchen in two panelled cupboards.

many of these fine pieces were absolutely essential for the business of eating, but once an 18th-century gentleman possessed them they became a necessity – an imposing means of impressing others as they viewed the finery by the light of the many candles in the new imposing candelabra.

So it must have been sometime after this that the dining room became established as the temple to status and ritual that it remained for the next 150 years. It rather seems that in many households by the end of the 19th century the idea of dining room meals being either a comfort, or indeed a pleasure, was thought quite alien, and by the mid 20th century it was not hard to still find, even in quite small houses, a cold dining room shut off from the world, dominated by a vast, empty but highly polished table and matching straight backed chairs – a room which said nothing of the pleasures of eating or entertaining. Thankfully, due in part to a general contraction of living space, as well as an increasingly more informal way of life for most of us, the old-fashioned, formal dining room is slowly becoming rarer and in fifty years the traditional dining room, in all its splendid isolation, will probably be looked at as a complete anachronism – as much part of another time as the ice-house or the ballroom.

But although formal dining may be decreasing, what is very much on the increase is the idea of enjoyable, social and sociable meals with friends, and so it is still a priority to have the right area in the house in which one can eat in comfort and with pleasure. This, of course, is exactly the sort of problem any interior decorator relishes – the effective manipulation of space – and so although the problems remain, the solutions are myriad. You may of course want, and have room for, a separate dining room with the dining table centre stage. If this is your preference, do not leave the table bare and forlorn: dress it during the day to give it a role as a display stage. A patterned cloth, or a long strip of an old textile down the centre, will break the bulk. Add a mixture of interesting and not dining-related pieces as well as vases and pots of flowers and greenery, remembering that the larger the table, the larger the scale of what you put on it should be. Using a cloth is the easiest way to change a dining table into something else, and modern decorators make full use of the many options available, which range from specially made floor-length cloths, either untrimmed or finished with fringing or passementerie to old textiles – on their own, or over other cloths – and combinations of both old and new.

Many people who entertain on a regular basis have embraced the idea – rather as in the mid-18th century – of having several small tables from which endlessly varied seating plans can be made. If the tables are of equal height they can be pushed together, or left in small groups. Some people prefer a choice of tables so that different permutations of numbers can sit

Everyone wants to eat in convivial surroundings, but each person's concept of conviviality is different. In an East Hampton holiday house the large kitchen gives plenty of room for an area containing a simple table and rustic chairs and purposely decorated with oversized striking objects – both antique and modern (far left).

In the very sunny south of France, Frédéric Méchiche keeps a cool corner of his sitting room as an eating area (above). A simple metal table and chairs is set off by a rare ceramic char-coal burner of the Directoire period – sitting on a commode.

This tiny dining room is furnished in consciously neoclassical vein, softened with a blue and white striped table-cloth, and carefully distressed walls which give the look of distemper (left).

Any space can be the right space for dining. In this Mississippi plantation house, Vicente Wolf has cleverly made part of the vast hall which runs the length of the house into a dining area (right). The round dining table is counteracted by the rectilinear design of the staircase and precisely hung pictures.

In this imposing and wonderful Paris dining room, designed by Yves Gastou (below), with its 18th-century panelling still in its original colour, it was bold but successful to use a table and chairs from the 1940s as well as a spectacular green-toned Venetian glass chandelier.

Scale is everything: in a small room, a large dining table looks far better than an insignificant one (below right). The eclectic mix – Eastern chairs, an Indian tablecloth, an early American painted fireboard and sepia photographs – are all perfectly harmonious.

Laura Bohn perfectly demonstrates how to combine both old and new – a contemporary table with chairs of different ages – in her country dining room (bottom) as well as how to put together a harlequin set. Each chair is different, yet all work together.

In this London dining room East meets West in a most reflective mood – reflected and brought together by the recurring blue and white theme as well as the unusual, translucent celadon-green glazed walls (right).

Vienna Sezessionstil dining chairs are combined with a modern glass-topped dining table through which the woven rug – an abstract design by Sonia Delaunay – makes its own strong statement (opposite below).

down. (Tables do not of course have to be a major investment. Even a trestle table can work perfectly well if covered with a cloth.)

For others, an option is to have an eating area within, but distinct from, either the kitchen or the main living room. If you take this route, do not fall into the trap of making the area just a new version of your old dining room – it should be very much part of the rest of the room but appear inviting, welcoming, a place where eating, when it happens, will evidently be a pleasure. Those who own large kitchens often glamorize one end so that eating in the kitchen moves away from the 1960's idea of taking 'potluck in the kitchen' (whatever that was supposed to be) and makes one end almost an informal dining room – very often with an antique table, and equally often with assorted chairs, both old and new. Such an arrangement of chairs – which gives an instantly relaxed, rather than formal, feeling to a table – will work as long as all the chairs are of roughly the same height and shape. Some may be with arms and some without, but it is best if they are all of the

In the summer heat of Tuscany, a cool dining area is an absolute necessity. This room is painted in iced melon and sports a dramatic candelabra (left).

Irene and Giorgio Silvagni in Provence eat in a room where doors open either end onto cool courtyards (above). The muted forest and earth colours are the key to the pleasure and charm of this room.

same basic design – round or straight backed, for example. Upholstered-backed chairs do not as a rule mix terribly well with those with wooden backs. While on the subject of dining chairs, although traditionally they were straight backed and relatively formal, there is no reason why small armchairs of the right height might not be used, nor indeed straight-backed winged or reading chairs. A small sofa or a high-backed settle against the wall are other options which can be very convivial when you have friends sitting and talking while dinner is prepared.

Another way of utilizing space, which is very much of our time, is to have a dining table, often a round one, permanently kept in a room which has also several other uses – a room with bookshelves and books for reading, or a room with tools for working. During the day – and indeed all the time the table is not in dining use – it may be covered with a cloth; it will certainly have flowers, plants, piles of books and other favourite objects and ornaments placed upon it.

Perhaps because objects and furnishings are seen from a seated point of view, the eye enjoys symmetry in the dining room more than in any other room in the house – but it should not be the sort of symmetry where everything matches exactly. The symmetry should be underneath the decorative veneer; better a symmetry of scale, with a large mass on one side of the room, say, matched by a mass of equal density on the other side. Scale and its synonym, proportion, are the secret of successful decoration. Most designers start with scale and from that point take risks. As Alidad remarked, if you put furniture of the wrong scale into a room nothing you could do consequently will work. Scale used properly, however, can have all manner of effects in a room, including appearing to make walls recede and the space become larger.

If the area where you eat is to have more than one personality – perhaps an office during the day – then evening lighting is of the utmost importance; it is perhaps more influential here than in any other room. Comfortable dining is about atmosphere, and an atmosphere is created with good lighting. Who has not felt uneasy at a table lit only by an overhead light that casts its flat glare over everything? Traditionally, candlelight was the preferred form of illumination, and there are many people even today who would not think of dining without a candlestick or candelabra. It is true that the flickering light of candles tends to enwrap everything – guests and furniture – in soft gauzy tones which make the best of what there is, and throw textiles and wall colour into romantic relief.

However, if you feel you need more than candlelight, a combination of lighting works well, and one of the simplest ways of mixing periods is to use state-of-the-art background lighting with specific lamps of different styles: recessed downlighters, uplighters and so on, with other lights set at places round the room to create specific areas of light. Needless to say, dimmers are imperative in a dining room – there are moments, such as when guests take their seats, when focused lighting is necessary and then there are other moments when the softer the gleam the better the evening.

Finally, remember a dining table does not always have to have the same setting. Different tablecloths – both undercloths and top cloths – china, glass and silverware can give the table as many different personae as you have occasion for: formal, informal, cheerful, romantic. Nor do the china or glass have to match. Colour or shape can be the overriding theme – all blue glass, or red-and-white china. It all helps to make eating a friendly pursuit, and that, after all, is the aim of the exercise.

Christopher Hodsoll, in his London house (right), takes an imposing room and furniture and overlays on this formal structure objects, paintings – each quirky, each interesting, each something to study.

Bathrooms and Kitchens

Whilst most of the other important rooms in houses are regarded today in much the same way that they were 200 years ago, what we expect from those two poor relations, the kitchen and the bathroom, has changed dramatically. Mere function is no longer sufficient. Now not only must they perform with efficiency, they must also please the eye of the beholder – and the beholder's friends. Imagination and a decorative twist is called for.

Only Frédéric Méchiche could create such an impossibly smart bathroom, with its massive antique iron bath and the 20th-century perspex chairs placed either side to act as towel holders as well as seating (left). The painted panels add even more glamour.

In this Swedish-inspired guest house (above) even the simple sink has been made into a decorative object which is a pleasure to behold.

Old and new, East and West all meet in a tiny London bathroom decorated by Prue Lane (below). Uniformly pale colours and tongue-and-groove boards make the small space appear larger.

A clever bathroom is placed in part of the bedroom where the ceiling slopes down (centre right). Pieces of very un-bathroom like furniture give it a unique charm.

Christopher Gibbs has converted this antique chair into what could literally be called a throne (bottom right).

This bathroom has a story to tell (right and far right). The huge gilt mirror, floor-length heavy curtains, 1930's stool and free-standing basin make an intriguing room in the Salvagni bastide in France.

Almost severe in their architectural detail are this wash-stand, heavy mirror and bold wall lights (below far right).

A bathroom to spend time in: a warm tiger-printed rug, chest of drawers and stained wood cabinet create a welcoming atmosphere (opposite page right).

are so modern and high tech – power showers, whirlpool jet baths, heated mirrors, extractor fans and so on – it is still strangely enough a very good room in which to inject an element of the antique or the unusual. Many people, for example, prefer large Victorian- or Edwardian-style basins, with their wide surrounding ledges and capacious bowls, and high-sided roll-top free-standing baths.

In the same way the kitchen is becoming more of an all-purpose living room and less of a clinical laboratory, so the bathroom today need not be a symphony of built-in vanitory units (whatever that means) and easy-to-wipe surfaces. It *can* have comfortable chairs, in

Today's bathroom can easily become a sort of modern treasure house, crammed with all manner of things that would be lost elsewhere in the house. There might be small pictures and prints, hung closely; or mirrors – old, small ones which do not have much of a practical use on their own but which look terrific when massed together on a wall, giving a many-faceted reflection. Soap and toothbrushes and paste can be kept in those odd saucers, cups and dishes which are too pretty to throw away. Combining charming objects and furniture in this way, the whole room can become a veritable bathroom cabinet of curiosities.

The perceived notion of the kitchen throughout most of our own century, like the bathroom, has been of somewhere where sterile hygiene has been substituted for charm. The only permissible decoration was gleaming storage jars filled with wholesome foods, so at first thought the kitchen does not seem a particularly appropriate place to provide the opportunity to decorate with antiques, or anything else much.

But kitchens used to be familiar cosy rooms as well as being practical and remarkably efficient. The inevitable open fire contributed to the feeling of aesthetic pleasure, as did the copper pans and moulds and an abundance of seasonal food. A central table dominated the room, and a dresser and cupboard held everything needed by the cook. Medieval and later paintings show kitchens decorated with pieces of pewter, bowls, dishes, pitchers, wooden utensils and platters of vegetables and other foods piled onto tables and dressers. The functional provided the visual.

which you can sit and chat; or a pretty stool that can double up as an extra surface on which to keep towels to hand; small attractive chests of drawers to store clean towels, or to act as a base in which to sink a basin; and a free-standing magazine rack or small decorative bookshelf for essential bathroom reading. Unusual wall-mounted cabinets and cupboards that are too small to hold anything of great size in other rooms in the house find a natural home in the bathroom, containing those myriad toiletries we all amass in their various bottles, jars and packets.

Texture is important in the bathroom to add warmth and luxury. This can be achieved with the addition of curtains or blinds – made from fabric that is not over susceptible to steam and damp – or it may be with a carpet or rug on the floor. There could be a pretty screen to keep away any small draughts or to modestly conceal the lavatory or bath from view. The bath or shower, if it is not enclosed, can be draped in sheer fabrics – always lined, of course, with a separate plastic waterproof curtain.

In a bathroom in her Connecticut barn (opposite), Bunny Williams has put together unusual fixtures and objects to create contrasting textures: fluted marble columns support a shaped slate basin with its modern stainless-steel plumbing on display, and a faceted Venetian glass mirror is hung on the rough clapboard wall.

This charming arrangement illustrates that, with flair, all styles and periods can be used together in a bathroom (above).

Julie Prisca designed this ingenious and practical free-standing basin unit in iron (right). It includes open shelves to keep everything at hand.

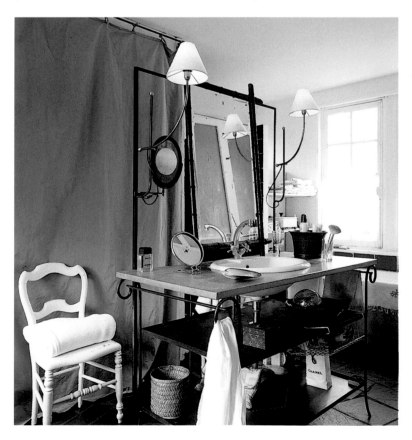

What seems to be happening now in kitchens is that there is a reaction against the trend for impersonal functionality of recent years: our pure wide-eyed wonder at the science of kitchen design and the interest in excessive hygiene is over. Our initial enthusiasm for the novelty of space-age kitchens has diminished, and perhaps we have finally decided all that professional-grade equipment can be left to the chef working in his restaurant-sized kitchen with his army of helpers, catering for huge numbers of people, not just family and friends.

The nicest kitchens these days seem to be those that are not just food laboratories behind serried ranks of closed-door units, but those which incorporate an element of real life as well. Kitchens should be about pleasure and relaxation, eating and entertaining, and as the dining room recedes in importance, the kitchen becomes an even more important place to spend pleasant times, while still incorporating a certain efficiency. One of the easiest ways to do this is to incorporate furniture which was not particularly designed for that room, such as

A huge, antique butcher's block is the central feature in this kitchen (above).

Frank Faulkner has put everything he likes into the kitchen in his Hudson house, including oil paintings, a chest of drawers and an antique balloon chair (below left).

Modern efficiency in the shape of a wooden island unit combines with antique comfort in the table, chairs and antique American cupboard (below right).

This old kitchen has not been modernized in any way, merely decorated (opposite). Everything is to hand, works efficiently and looks charming.

comfortable chairs, an upholstered armchair, a small sofa, or perhaps a table which is from a different, earlier period sitting in front of a row of contemporary units – which often look best painted to tone with the older furniture.

As in the dining room, there is no need for the chairs all to match each other: a harlequin set – as long as each chair is of the similar sort of proportions – can look very inviting. If you are planning to mix periods or styles in the kitchen, the worktops should not be overly clinical in appearance. Wood looks and feels good and is wonderfully neutral in style; if you prefer a harder surface, choose something dark-toned like granite or slate.

Utensils and cooking pans borrowed from other cultures and other periods can have an immediate charm, and their patina and finish, and sometimes bright colours, add depth and interest to the most mundane of shelves. Pictures can and should be hung on kitchen walls, and rugs used on cold kitchen floors. Efficiency does not have to dictate a dearth of creature comforts and pleasures.

Bedrooms

More than any other room in the house, the bedroom is the most private, and therefore says the most about you and the way you like to live. Whatever its style, it reflects with sharp accuracy your personality. Informal, formal? Cold or warm? This is the moment for a little decorative self-analysis.

This bedroom is tiny, but it looks much bigger because of the way the bed is dressed and the ceiling-hung canopy is draped (left). The rope accentuates the composition.

The bed in this room sits at some distance from the wall, allowing flowers and decorative objects to be arranged around it (above).

The more gruelling the outside world appears, the more the bedroom is perceived as a place of sanctuary – set apart from more functional spaces. As well as the usual utilitarian considerations, adornment, decoration and comfort are all vital requisites in a modern bedroom. The mood matters: it must be a pleasant mood, one with a personality. The colours must be pleasing, to you if to no one else, and the designs appropriate. It is a place where your most personal possessions, those things which you like to see every day, should be displayed. It is a room of options.

In an age when a bedroom of one's own is considered a necessity rather than a luxury, and the idea of sleeping with several other adults or a combination of adults and children is for many people perceived at best as a curiosity, it is interesting to recall that once the bed – originally just a thin mattress in an alcove in the Great Hall – had been moved out of the communal space into a separate room in about the 12th century, it was several hundred more years before it was considered even slightly desirable to take the concept of privacy any further and provide each adult member of the household with his or her own bedroom. The main bedroom housed the lord and his family, while other members of the household still slept within the hall itself, where the central fireplace, the

Robert Kime mixes pattern, texture and textiles to create a totally calm and comfortable bedroom (below).

An antique American bed is combined with an Indian bedspread and curtain, with a Victorian footstool (below).

Laura Bohn in Pennsylvania hangs a traditional four-poster in soothing soft green draperies (below right).

This colonial bed has bedhead hangings in modern toile de Jouy, the design taken from 18th-century documents (below).

only source of heat, warmed them. The concept of privacy only evolved – and that incredibly slowly – as daily life became less of a struggle for survival, and other priorities were able to come to the fore. Once the idea of a separate bedroom was finally and firmly established, the bed as a structure in its own right began to take shape. Eventually the bed itself became one of the most important pieces of furniture in the house. It was dressed with precious hangings; costly status symbols in themselves, their importance reflected in turn on the whole bedroom, which began to assume an importance shared by no other room.

By the 17th century, in the Low Countries, the principal bedroom was often furnished as a comfortable all-purpose reception room, with the bed just part of the furniture. The bed itself was usually closed off and either built into the wall or with curtains completely enclosing the bed, close-fitted to the frame and reaching to the ground. In other parts of Europe, however, bedrooms were often still small chambers off larger rooms and used solely for sleeping. Separate sets of bed hangings were made for summer and for winter – heavy woven tapestries, embroidered velvets and damasks for the colder months and lighter-weight silks and even cottons for summer – particularly in southern countries.

The porcelain posts and antique silk hangings on this bed need no extra embellishment, old or new (below left).

To complement the mixture of a domed four-poster and Chinese chairs, chests and pots, the hangings are simple (below).

Undeniably, old beds do have their disadvantages, such as lumpy, sloping mattresses or odd-sized bases that modern fitted sheets resolutely do not fit. But they can also have unique charm and are often decorated in a fashion not easy to find in a contemporary bed. But if you really cannot live without the modern comforts of a new bed or cannot find something acceptable in the antique field, then consider making a new bed more individual, either with what you put behind it, on it or in front of it.

In most rooms, a bed covered in a plain colour or single pattern is too much for the eye to handle, and boring to boot. Looking down onto the

bed – which is what one inevitably tends to do with modern beds, which are so much lower than antique ones – it is good to see some form or design, an interruption in the density. One way of breaking the monotony of an expanse of bed covering is to place a long stool, ottoman or chest at the foot of the bed. A chaise longue, day bed or low sofa can also be effective, but remember the back should not be higher than a footboard would be. If the room is not large enough for such furniture, cover the end of the bed with a piece of contrasting textile, either folded over flat or in handkerchief point, or a blanket or folded quilt.

Indeed, if you love old textiles, the bed is the perfect place to show them off – small pieces can be incorporated in a panelled bedhead, a larger piece into sham pillows to sit on the bed during the day. Narrow bed hangings can be made from old curtains suspended from rods set into the wall, and a corona attached to the wall or ceiling can also be draped with relatively narrow pieces of old fabric. An old patchwork quilt (even the

Christophe Gollut's antique bed is a statement: standing alone in the room, it takes full advantage of the round bay window and is surrounded by all one could need (opposite).

A small simple Tuscan bedroom is brought to life with a set of antique arboreal prints above it (left).

Christopher Hodsoll has designed a contemporary, classical bedroom that includes antique and modern (below left). The perspex table lamps and the bedside cabinets are to his own design.

It is a lucky baby who sleeps in this room, complete with antique cupboard, Moroccan lantern and a leather rug on which to crawl (below).

some furnishings which can be changed around to alter the look and the feel between the different seasons. This is not as difficult as it sounds when using textiles. It could be a different bed cover – perhaps starched, white linen in the summer and a heavy damask in the winter – or simply the addition of different pieces of antique textiles over a basic bed cover – an appliquéd or embroidered shawl in the summer, a woollen paisley or an Indian shawl or northern plaid in the winter.

The once ubiquitous bedroom suites are no longer the sought-after items they once were – which, on balance, can only be a good thing. The picture of matching piece after matching piece of heavy, usually dark-stained, wooden furniture – plodding wardrobe, heavy bed, a chest of

largest of which are usually smaller than the area of most modern beds), a paisley shawl, an old plaid blanket, antique lace, a tribal blanket – the bed is the best excuse ever to display a favourite piece of textile.

It is rare that a bedhead that exactly matches the bed linen is effective. The bedhead need not (dare one say, should not) be shiny and quilted or padded and covered. Instead, it provides an opportunity to imaginatively utilize any number of unusual textiles or materials, and other pieces of the same type of fabric used on the bedhead can also be used as hangings. The bedhead can be of another design entirely of course: upholstered, perhaps, or painted in contrast to the bed itself. A piece of panelling or painted canvas, a half-height screen, a quilt or shawl stiffened with padding and hung from wooden battens – all these are options.

If the bed hangings are original to an old bed or were made to be in keeping with its period, then take a colour from those and use it for the rest of the room, but in a simple, uncluttered way. If the bed does not have its original hangings, consider using the simplest of contemporary textiles – white muslin, unlined undyed silk or calico would be a clean contrast to the mass of the bed. This applies equally to the dressing of bedroom windows – if the bed is antique and stands out, keep the curtains and blinds as simple and plain as you can.

These ideas are ways to make a bedroom feel comfortable – which is important: it should feel womb-like and comforting but also, conversely, airy and light. In winter cosiness and snugness are what one desires; in the summer months, open windows and light breezes – so consider having

Although the table and bed in this interesting group are actually very different (left), the fact that they are both made of metal gives a cohesive lightness and charm to the room.

This room has been put together in a way that is reminiscent of another time (below). A once-white bed, assorted cushions, early 20th-century sports equipment and a few dead beasts and fowls make it a countryman's room.

drawers and often a dressing table to boot – was neither a cheering nor a restful sight, but resembled more an over-fitted kitchen. Today, the prettiest bedrooms are often those furnished with many different pieces of furniture, such as a light chair or a delicate painted chest of drawers. Bedrooms are the places to display all those slightly more fragile, often frivolous single pieces that you cannot resist, but which may be overlooked in other, more serious rooms. And although traditionally in the West, the bed is usually ranged with its head against a wall, there is no particular reason for this; in a large room the bed, particularly if it is interesting in shape, can float in the centre of the room.

Many bedrooms are small, however, and therefore the perfect place to practise the art of using scale correctly. This concept, so often discussed by decorators, is the idea of using large pieces rather than small ones in a small space. A bed in itself is large: in a small bedroom, treat it with

Once again the power of a single colour to link different objects is skilfully demonstrated (above). White is almost always best for this – it flatters and unites.

aplomb and make the most of it rather than attempting to minimize its bulk. Wall colour is also important in a small bedroom. Note the example of French designer Annie Kuentzman-Levet, who decorated a room, so small that there was barely enough room for us to set up the camera, in an exuberant Indian Tree of Life design; covered the bed in red checked fabric; and artfully hung another textile over a beam for an informal canopy. The result is a warm,room that invites rest and relaxation. All bedrooms *should* be warm and welcoming. Obviously, this does not mean that in a sunny climate they should be carpeted and decorated in tones of red and pink. But what it does mean is that the colours should be soft rather than strident, calm rather than busy. Lines should be gentle, the colours you choose muted.

Lighting is important in a bedroom, far more important than is often realized. If you have tables beside the bed, any bedside lights on them must be tall enough to actually throw some light on reading matter. Practically speaking they should also be fitted with switches at the door as well as on the lights. If you have a four-poster bed, arranging reading lights is not quite as easy as with a divan bed, as the curtains can obscure the light from a bedside lamp. One solution, if the posts of the bed are thick

Irene and Giorgio Silvagni have a bedroom that is a triumph of pattern, texture and colour (opposite). The upholstered bed, the deep blue mosquito net, the quilt-covered armchair and the incongruous leopard-print chairs all combine extremely sympathetically.

In a dovecote, deep strong colour unites and makes a guest room from a fairly basic space (above left).

In another Silvagni bedroom, an antique bed is combined with 20th-century furniture and a bench that is neoclassical in style (above).

This bed in East Hampton has Swedish, Indian and American overtones (left). A chequerboard design on rush matting on the floor echoes colours in the Indian quilt and curtains.

enough, is to fix the sort of swing-arm reading lamps (usually made of brass) that are normally secured to the wall behind the bed to the posts themselves, inside the curtains.

Many people like a central ceiling light to act as a 'house light' in a bedroom. This is the ideal place for a pretty decorative lamp or, even better, for a chandelier. Placed above the bed,

In artist Frank Faulkner's Manhattan loft bedroom (above), everything is pulled together by the richly patterned and textured wall, which is actually sections of paint-splattered plywood from his studio floor.

Annie Kuentzman-Levet demonstrates the principle of using a large scale pattern in a small room by papering this tiny bedroom in Normandy in an all-flowing, exuberant Indian Tree of Life design, which gives a warm unity to the tiny room (right).

you get the bonus of gazing upwards and fully appreciating the art of the chandelier, viewing as you do the crystal drops and swags from a supine vantage point. On a practical level, dimmers for every light, whether free-standing or fixed, are essential in a bedroom.

If your bedroom is a mixture of old and new, consider having a dressing table – once an essential, now not always considered necessary. A pretty table to sit at, furnished with all that one might need to be beautiful, and furnished with a tall narrow table lamp or two and a pretty decorative mirror is a civilized addition to any bedroom, and far kinder to the face than clinically correct bare make-up bulbs arranged around an unframed glass.

Hallways and Landings

This landing is as interesting as the reception rooms in this house in Provence, and used to create a picture in perspective (above).

This small entrance hall in Tuscany has been decorated with as much care and attention to detail as any more important room (right).

Too many halls and landings are treated as purposeless, dead spaces and decorated with an unseeing eye. But halls and landings are not places for left-over junk for which you can find no other spot. Rather, they are legitimate opportunities for decoration – proper spaces where the design principles of proportion and harmony used throughout the rest of the house can be applied.

It may be a cliché, but the hall *is* the first thing people see when they enter a house, and it behoves you therefore to think carefully about how it should be decorated. It should be welcoming of course, but it should also give a taste of the delights beyond, the pleasures to be found in the other rooms in your home. So the look of it must reflect the decorative style of the rest of the house – whether it be dramatic, peaceful, or the style of a particular period. It should also, of course, work on a practical level, while not having the appearance of the place where old walking boots and torn coats go to die. Ideally, there should be hanging storage, a flat surface on which to place keys and letters, and a decent-sized mirror – this last an absolute necessity for both those who are arriving and those who are departing. A mirror will not only make the hall look larger; if it is antique and ornate – Venetian bevelled glass, perhaps, or framed in heavily gilded moulding – it will look particularly striking hung in a hall which has been painted in strong contemporary colours.

Many halls, particularly in tall narrow town houses, are long, confined and often dark. If there is little or no natural light, maximize the darkness by painting the walls in a strong dramatic colour, perhaps glazed to give a reflective quality. Do not economize on artificial lighting. Apart from the safety aspect, an ill-lit hall has a depressing effect, as well as taking away the impact of your carefully planned decorative scheme. If you want to have ceiling lights in the hall, consider using more than one. Two lights

In both halls and landings Christopher Gibbs demonstrates his taste and talent in the arrangement of rooms. An upper landing (far left) holds a central pyramid bookcase – an interesting use of what could be a wasted space. The inner hall (left) is a place to linger. The surround to the door at the entrance to the drawing room beyond has been painted a warm green to illustrate and frame the delights beyond. Even the outer hall (below) is a place to stop and look; everything has been chosen to give interest and amusement.

hung at each end of a narrow hall look far better, and give more specific light, than one hung centrally. Lanterns, perhaps with etched or coloured glass panes, or lamps which enclose the naked bulb, look far better than an open shade as you descend the stairs. If there is space, think of having a lamp on a small table. The soft light it gives is far more welcoming than merely having an overhead light. Instead of thinking of the hall as a throughway – a place that only leads to somewhere more interesting – think of the area as a room in its own right. Hallways and landings are spaces just as much as reception rooms, so do not waste the space; use a narrow one as a display case, a larger one as a modern ante-room.

People can look more closely at the furniture in these more intimate spaces than they would in larger rooms, so use decorative pieces – the sort of furniture that has no particular function, but is simply pretty. A wide or square hall always looks better with a piece of furniture positioned in the centre – a table, desk or even small sofa. It stops the entrance hall from looking as if the removal men have just been. Landings, particularly oddly shaped half-landings, are very often ignored, but this forced pause on the stairs provides an opportunity to hang a striking picture at eye level, or to place an object or piece of sculpture, or a chair with attitude. Landings ought to be decorated in such a way that they reflect the bedrooms beyond, not with things for which you can find no other use. Larger ones can often be fitted with book shelves, even in small and difficult corners, and filled with the sort of books which people like to read in bed.

The hall is also the place to show off your most unusual – not to say eccentric – pieces; objects that will benefit from being viewed at close quarters and will reward inspection: a striking group of pictures, a wall hanging, an ethnic costume in a long narrow hall; a painted table or even a statue in a wide hall. Decorators often use these spaces to put together carefully considered groups of decorative pieces, or even hang unlikely two-dimensional objects. Pictures are invaluable on a landing, and it is important not to forget the stairwell wall, which offers the space to hang

To come upon a hall like this is unexpected in a plantation house in Mississippi (opposite). Vicente Wolf has cleverly designed a space that is clean and calm – a refuge from the summer heat.

A landing in a beach house has had the space cleverly filled with a four-sided seat set in the middle, which sits around a central table, and a striking eccentrically dressed chandelier (below).

The cool colours used in this London apartment landing (right) reflect the calm of the bedroom beyond.

Only a place of such natural grandeur as this 18th-century Paris apartment, decorated by Yves Gastou (below right), could accommodate such a strong group of 20th-century furniture and artefacts.

A simple seating area has been created on this landing (left), with views both ways to the garden beyond.

A hall that leads to the garden (below) is furnished in the manner of a delightful room, part library, part cabinet of curiosities.

This simple arrangement combines the necessary – hats and besom brooms – with the decorative – paintings and a tapestry-backed chair (right).

something large – if not a traditional painting, perhaps an old textile or a series of photographic prints that have been enlarged, and then mounted and framed with a uniform design. Even a collection of objects could be suspended on the stair walls, provided they cannot easily be knocked – large shells, say, or old toys or farming implements. All these things will lead the eye upwards and distract the thoughts from the narrowness of what is below. Build up rather than down. The more ornate the objects and pictures you have on display, the simpler should be the wall and floor decoration. This is modern and of our time.

The floor, particularly in a narrow hall, has a critical importance. Wood, stone, marble or tiles are options – with or without rugs. The floor should look good and be easy to clean; cream carpet is not a wise choice. The hall flooring should also connect with the floor treatment of the staircase. Uncarpeted stairs can be decorated with a design on the risers, or the risers can be painted a different colour from the treads.

A hall in New Jersey contrasts the simplicity of a rough-boarded wall with the sophistication of an antique Irish table, a collection of bronzes and a finely carved mirror (above).

An open staircase can sometimes look lost but Bunny Williams has pulled it together with animal-inspired charm – both in paintings and standing below the stairs (opposite).

Garden Rooms

Although early conservatories – those built in the 18th and 19th centuries – could be very grand and glamorous, the late 20th-century renaissance in this most useful of additions often concentrated more on making the space an extension of the indoor area, instead of giving it a personality and identity of its own – neither inside nor outside, but a magic limbo all of its own. This is the place where fantasy, rather than practicality, should reign supreme.

American decorator Bunny William's conservatory in Connecticut is truly grand, with an inspired use of larger-than-life scale to make the point (left and above). Here grand gestures are the norm.

There is an enormous sense of release and relaxation in a garden room – a room which may be anything from a glassed-in porch to a fully fledged, centrally heated conservatory and which is either attached to the house or built as a separate building elsewhere in the garden. One's spirit is invariably raised when inside one of these light-filled structures. Perhaps it is the idea that one is almost outside, practically in the garden, but that one is somehow cheating the elements by using an enclosed room, so avoiding any of the annoyances of the great outdoors.

The conservatory grew out of the orangery, where tender plants, particularly citrus fruits, were sheltered during the winter. New building

techniques allowed the iron-framed, glass-paned constructions to soar to new heights during the 19th century. Architecturally, the king of the conservatory was the 6th Duke of Devonshire's head gardener, Joseph Paxton (1801–65), who designed not only the Great Conservatory at Chatsworth House in Derbyshire (which at 37 metres was wide enough for Queen Victoria to ride through it in her carriage and pair) but also the Crystal Palace, home of the Great Exhibition of 1850. Such amazing structures spawned many smaller, but to their owners equally magical, conservatories, and by the end of the 19th century they were attached to many a moderate home, where they were used mainly for raising plants.

Today, the conservatory is enjoying a renaissance and is seen very much as part of the house, usually with a door which gives direct access to inside. No longer a storage place for broken-down deck chairs and dead tomato plants, the conservatory has entered the vocabulary of domestic decoration and many people now see them really as garden rooms – effortlessly linking the interior with the garden beyond, and used most often as a sunny morning room or a light-filled dining room.

Although in all these garden rooms there are often plants and shrubs in tubs and pots, the gardening element is on the whole more decorative than seriously horticultural. But decorative or not, plants are important in

A conservatory can be an integral part of the house, as is John Rosselli's in New Jersey (far left). Complete with birds in and out of cages, it links the dining room and drawing room.

Robert Kime's old sunny conservatory, in which plants – climbers, shrubs and flowers – grow in random colourful profusion around the appropriately sturdy table and chairs, is illuminated by a collection of lanterns and, of course, an exuberant chandelier (left).

An outdoor dining room or loggia in Italy, with rough-cast concrete walls (above), has been painted with almost imperceptible broad stripes of green colourwash that change during the day as they reflect the light, making an ever-changing background.

any conservatory – they accentuate the connection between inside and out in this transitional space, and act as a taster of the more verdant delights beyond. Containers can be as varied as the plant life: traditional terracotta flower pots, yes, but also some more unexpected containers – anything from old copper preserving pans to patterned china foot baths, stone troughs and basins, or even an old wooden trunk.

Garden rooms make the best of what sunshine there is – they capture it, keep it and extend it, and at night they reflect the sky and all within it. So furniture and furnishings should reflect this outdoors feeling, with no heavy upholstery, dark wood or winter warmers. This sort of room offers an excuse to exercise the most elaborate sort of fantasies where decor is concerned. Responsible to no one and following no pattern, the garden

This variation on the outdoor room is an enclosed porch (opposite). The outer porch (left) is made remarkable by the exotic table and the plant made of tin.

Antique garden tools are appropriate decoration in this potting shed (below).

Lars Bolander uses a sunny terrace as the perfect outdoor room, complete with every comfort (below left).

As plantation dwellers have always done, the owners of this Mississippi house (bottom) enjoy the view from a hammock.

room can be a bejewelled and colourful Eastern souk, a classical marble or stone temple, a leafy forest glade, a repository for natural curiosities – or even all of those things together. Such a room responds to light-hearted furniture: the witty, the fantastic and the amusing. And so many different types of pieces can be used in the conservatory – not only stools, comfortable seats and benches, but also sometimes rugs and mats on the floor, lanterns and lights, to say nothing of the vital dining table and chairs. Garden rooms are places where many different styles, objects and, above all, textures can be mixed. Natural looking materials – such as wood, wicker, raffia and bamboo – real or false, are the best. Tables can be stone or marble, metal add an element of warmth and cosiness. The warmer the prevailing climate, the cooler can be the conservatory. Outdoor rooms in hot countries – more loggias than conservatories – can be enhanced by a judicious use of colour.

As far as finding the right thing to cover some of the glass, this is definitely not the place for fussy curtain treatments or fancy blinds.

Annie Kuentzman-Levet, in Normandy, constructs a *herisson* or hedgehog on which to store her antique flower pots (above).

In Christopher Gibbs's conservatory, the antique bath, filled with rain water, is set off by the colourful stained-glass panel, the round wooden seated chair and, of course, the luxuriant plants (above right).

or even pre-cast concrete, made to look more natural with a roughened appearance.

Any conservatory which is to be used for dining should be warm and friendly. It is no great thrill to eat in a glass house simply because it is a glass house, and they can be cold. Rugs on the floor and plenty of cushions on the chairs

Special translucent pull-down roller blinds that insulate and shade when necessary are now available for conservatories. Blinds made from split cane or rattan also convey the right look.

Conservatories are great places for mixing different styles of lighting: multi-coloured Moroccan glass lanterns, candles, Victorian coloured-glass fairy lights, 19th-century cut-glass candelabra, iron chandeliers – the more the merrier, and the more welcoming.

Outdoor seating has a charm of its own, and many of the designs would work well inside the house. Flights of fancy have included the woven paper Lloyd Loom chairs, strange twig chairs and upright wooden wing chairs, as well as the

totally inappropriate white plastic tubs on legs that are found in gardens everywhere today). Materials varied from cast and wrought iron to wire and steel; every sort of hard wood; wicker and cane as well as stone and marble. Very good antique garden furniture is very fashionable today, and therefore correspondingly expensive, but it is perfectly possible to buy slightly more

the house, inevitably, for those days when a trek to the bottom of the garden would be less than pleasant, but also scattered in more unexpected places, as they did when designing gardens in the 18th century that constituted almost an afternoon's excursion, complete with edifying texts and inspirational verses. A seat overlooking a view; a bench set off by the darkness of the

perennially popular rocking chair, seen on as many outdoor porches as in sitting rooms.

Over the centuries, much thought has been given to designing and making outdoor seating that would be in keeping with or in contrast to its surroundings (happily though, not in quite as much contrast as the near-ubiquitous and

utilitarian but still unusual and often unique pieces. They work anywhere, with new pieces (except the hated white plastic), indoors or out (much old garden furniture should be over-wintered inside, in any event).

In the garden, select places for interesting furniture that are not completely obvious; near

Bunny Williams dresses a conservatory in a dramatic, structural way. Even the terracotta pot and plant seem part of a decorative scheme (above left).

A large panel of tiles in Robert Kime's conservatory forms a focus on the house wall, which is flattered by freely growing geraniums (above top).

An outdoor porch on Long Island contrasts glass, metal and wood in a peaceful setting (above).

foliage of the hedge behind it, a group of chairs beside a sweet-smelling shrub or herbaceous border – as in the interior, think about each chair, bench or table as an object in its own right, not merely a functional item, and you will soon realize their potential for contributing to the overall decorative effect in the garden just as much as in the house.

No need for outdoor furniture to be any less attractive or comfortable than its interior equivalent. In Italy, this cushioned bench seems most inviting (top).

Garden furniture in stone, even if it is not old, should be allowed and indeed encouraged to weather (top centre).

An undersized cast-iron suite, complete with its own swinging chandelier, sits underneath a tree (top far right).

These antique fern-design iron seats have been so placed as to seem part of the garden growing around them (above).

Laura Bohn has put together an eclectic group of chairs around a wooden table, all anchored by an oversized lantern (right)

In front of an early American wood shingled cottage, an antique bench and a fine Windsor chair sit companionably, looking much as they must have done 150 years ago (opposite).

Antique
Styles

Introduction

Major periods of interior decoration are usually called by a political era, a ruler's name or that of a reigning house or regime. Furniture styles are usually named after specific craftsmen or designers working within those periods. So Chippendale furniture, for example, was made during the Georgian period in England, Boulle during the reign of King Louis XIV

of France, and that of Phyfe during the Federal period in American history. It would, of course, be strange if there were not many cross-over styles of furniture, many grey areas where one so-called period merges into another, or one type of design. After all, nearly all the styles we know today are based on, inspired by, or derived from, however loosely, classical designs – whether furniture found in Ancient Egyptian tombs; carved onto Greek stone steles; or excavated, petrified, from the volcanic ash of

Pompeii and Herculaneum. No designer, for example, has ever bettered the most famous of Ancient Greek seat designs – the curved-leg *klismos* and the folding X-stool, and the shape of the Roman throne is still instantly recognizable today. But interior design and decoration would not be what they are, nor so interesting, without chronological and national variations and so below we give a brief *aide-mémoire* of some of the more influential furniture styles through the centuries.

This summer living room in East Hampton combines East and West, old and new, and even different periods in an exuberant and cheerful way (opposite). Soft colour and tone are the key, as well as a harmony of scale and proportion.

This room is dependent on an understanding of scale for its success (below). Some most disparate objects have been brought together – although all of them share a rural feeling, and it is their conjunction which shows the skill of the decorator, Annie Kuentzman-Levet.

English

Early English furniture was relatively rough and ready in style, either constructed to be portable so that it could travel with the household, or else built in such massive style that it could be moved by no one – legally or illegally. By the 16th century, the look of most furniture had changed little; early Tudor household life still revolved around the Great Hall, although there were some private family rooms where living and sleeping were combined. The furniture was constructed by a joiner and was often of panel-and-frame construction, sometimes with added carved decoration. Chests, stools, tables, settles, cupboards and the occasional chair were made either in oak, or other native woods such as walnut, ash or elm. The great bed, with its expensive hangings, was the most valuable piece of furniture, often bequeathed in wills.

Although Henry VIII did encourage Italian craftsmen, England was an isolated nation in comparison with the sophisticated city-states of Italy, and the thinking behind the Renaissance did not greatly affect the development of English furniture design; it was not really until the Restoration that English furniture displayed any of the baroque flamboyance so typical of the Continental Renaissance.

After the difficult years of the Civil War and the resultant Commonwealth, the accession of Charles II to the throne brought with it a new exuberance in every area of daily life, including furniture design, as craftsmen – some English, some European – adapted the styles of France and Italy to the English taste. With new designs came new timbers, some from France and Spain, some from the new colonies in America, and even some exotics, like ebony, from the Far East, and pieces were often also additionally embellished with silver, gold and tortoiseshell.

And so we come to perhaps England's finest decorative hour – the 18th century. The early 18th century espoused the classical principles of Andrea Palladio (1508-80); interiors became formal and restrained with pieces of furniture monumental in design, and often heavily carved and gilded, conceived by architect–designers like William Kent. This was the first flush of

Tudor furniture was heavy and ornamental, usually made of native oak (top). Tables were secured with stretchers.

The four-poster bed in the 17th century, carved and hung with woven and embroidered textiles, was often the most valuable piece of furniture in the house (left).

For many people, no finer pieces of furniture have been designed than those 18th-century pieces from such designers as Thomas Chippendale, Robert Adam, George Hepplewhite and Thomas Sheraton (below from left).

neoclassicism, and that which was to become sober and even severe later in the century was, in the middle of the 18th century in the hands of Robert Adam, a delight. Inspired by Roman and Greek motifs and designs, Adam and others like George Hepplewhite (d. 1786) and Thomas Sheraton, designed fine furniture of classical simplicity and graceful linear design, which was in turn interpreted by master cabinetmakers like Thomas Chippendale (1718–79).

The second phase of neoclassical design – that which came to be known as Regency style in England, Empire style in France and Federal in America – was considered more derived from the antique, more classically correct. As opposed to Adam's cheerfully feminine designs, it was masculine in style, featuring dark woods like rosewood, gilding and ornament that included griffins, sphinxes, weapons and trophies.

Among this progression of taste there were also fashionable blips in furniture style: usually European in origin, they metamorphosed in a peculiarly English way. The Rococo style, for example, which in the rest of Europe was a sinuous, serpentine explosion, in England was manifested in neo-Gothic style – a prettified form loosely based on the original medieval Gothic architecture; chinoiserie, too – inspired by the architecture of China and Japan – was

This **18th-century table** shows the restrained elegant lines and carved and gilded decoration that are so typical of the period (above).

A fine 19th-century neo-Gothic chair is used as a hall chair (above).

The Windsor chair, in all its different decorative guises, has never lost its popularity (bottom row).

The Rococo, so popular on the continent, manifested itself in England in modified forms like Chippendale's chinoiserie style (centre right).

interpreted in England in gentler manner than in other countries, although the Prince Regent's Pavilion at Brighton – a bit Indian on the exterior and very Chinese on the interior – could hardly be described as gentle.

After around 1830, the choice of designs became wider than could have been imagined a hundred years earlier. European cities were now prosperous centres of consumer consumption, and the demand for new furniture was great. The results of this increased demand were not always propitious – furniture was produced in a plethora of antique styles, which ranged from medieval Gothic to a version of Queen Anne, as well as 'Jacobethan' and Scottish baronial – this last exemplified in Sir Walter Scott's Scottish house, Abbotsford, a combination of olde Scotland and a fairytale landscape. Perhaps the most successful style was the medieval Gothic revival, and it was shown at its best in the work of Augustus Welby Pugin, who based his work on original, pure Gothic architecture, rather

than a hotchpotch of medieval styles which coloured the commercial versions.

There were others as well as Pugin who wished for a return to what they saw as 'real design'. One of the most influential of these was William Morris, who founded a design and manufacturing company in 1861, developing from Pugin's medievalist base that which Morris called simple workaday furniture with an emphasis on craftsmanship, which eschewed the unnecessary ornamentation of the past and was in many ways based on rural tradition. From philosophies like these was born the Arts and Crafts movement – a reaction against standardization and commercial design – and Craftsmens' Guilds were formed, like The Art Workers Guild of 1884.

Also fashionable from about the 1860s, and also heavily influenced by Pugin's work, was the partly Japanese-inspired Aesthetic Movement. Designers such as William Burges (1827–81) and William Godwin (1833–86) introduced

The exaggeratedly elongated designs of Scotsman Charles Rennie Mackintosh represented the Art Nouveau style in early 20th-century Britain (left).

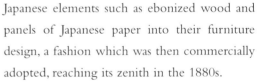

There is something solid and comforting in the distinctive clean lines and sharp angles of these chairs designed in the 1950s (below left).

Japanese elements such as ebonized wood and panels of Japanese paper into their furniture design, a fashion which was then commercially adopted, reaching its zenith in the 1880s.

Arts and Crafts ideals led, at the beginning of the 20th century, to what was to be known as Art Nouveau. Art Nouveau in Britain was once again very different from the European version, and was perhaps epitomized by the deeply personal style of Scottish architect Charles Rennie Mackintosh (1868–1928) whose influence was world wide and whose straight linear furniture is still instantly recognizable today. Working mostly in Scotland, Mackintosh developed a purely personal form of furniture design which combined elements of the swirls of European Art Nouveau, with the geometric lines of the Vienna Sezessionstil movement, as well as the honest traditions of English Arts and Crafts.

European

By the late 16th century the influence of the Renaissance movement was such that French and Italian craftsmen were designing decorative and decorated furniture of much exuberance and style, with a confidence which could not fail to influence other more northerly nations. Although this furniture was very beautiful, it was not until the 17th century that pieces were conceived individually, rather than as part of an architectural scheme. French furniture began to differ from that of the Italians in this regard. It enjoyed royal patronage, and a manufactory to supply royal palaces and promote a national style was established at the Gobelins in Paris.

Louis XIV – whose lengthy reign from 1643 to 1715 altered so much in France – was instrumental in changing the way decorative art was perceived. Most commissions stemmed from the Sun King or his circle, and craftsmen and artists gravitated towards the luxurious,

Early French 18th-century furniture had a charm and a grace that transcends the centuries (above).

French Renaissance furniture was often heavily carved and ornamented with a sophistication not seen in Northern Europe (below).

The great French furniture maker Georges Jacob (1739–1814) designed this model of elegance and simplicity – the essence of the 18th century (left).

The flowing lines and elaborate designs of the French Rococo style were enormously influential across the whole of Europe (above).

claustrophobic life at Versailles. Furniture of this period had a monumental quality and dazzling richness. Gilded wood, carved with flora, fauna, and the royal signature sunburst motif, shone.

After Louis XIV's death in 1715, the magnificence and grandeur of the past years began to give way to a new lightness and comfort. The 17th century saw continuous movement of craftsmen between the countries of Europe, which softened sharp national differences of taste. One reaction to the baroque authoritative style of Louis XIV was the Rococo. A sinuous, almost free, form of decoration that in its most extreme appearance spread its serpentine charms over furniture, walls and ceilings, it was warmly embraced in Italy and Germany, but, as usual, not so widely accepted in England.

Enthusiasm for, followed by reaction against, has always been the way of things – in fashion as in decoration – and there could not have been a much stronger reaction to what many saw as the extravagance of the Rococo than the discipline of neoclassicism. From its early start as *le gout grec* in the 1760s, it became a widely embraced style, lasting until the 1830s. Its form varied. The French version was affected by the political and human upheaval of the Revolution and its subsequent regimes. It was known as

Both the ornate chair (top left) and the sofa set on a stone cobbled floor and draped in traditional Provençal prints. (above), are typical Louis XVI.

This armless French chair (top right) is from the late 18th century, in the Directoire style.

The white painted table (top far right) is a simplified version of the Rococo.

Plain linen upholstery shows off the beautiful lines of this French Directoire armchair (right).

An austere linear Empire chest of drawers is embellished with such characteristic ornament as columns and gilded rosettes (centre right).

A simple Swedish chair of the 19th century (far right) continues in a long tradition of native folk art.

Empire style because the Emperor, Napoleon Bonaparte, was so influential in promoting and encouraging the style. He realized the benefits of identifying his regime with the glories of the past, as well as creating an enduring image for his new empire, demonstrating, as Louis XIV had done before him, France's power through her decorative arts. Empire style maintained a following well into the 19th century.

In the early 19th century, in Austria and Germany, *le style Empire* was reinterpreted as Biedermeier – a style that evolved from that of the Empire but in a far more comfortable and simple way that was almost domestic. The pieces were relatively low built, and distinctive in their light tones of cherry, pear and other native

The Vienna Sezessionstil was an Austrian version of Art Nouveau, which swept Europe (above left). The bentwood chair by Michael Thonet (1796–1871) is of the same period (above centre).

Biedermeier was a domestic German reaction to the flamboyance of Empire style (above).

This florid version of Art Nouveau uses stylized natural shapes in sinuous designs (right).

fruitwoods. The concept of their design was simple and far less ostentatious than the French or English neoclassical equivalents.

Then, in the 1890s, from many sources came the widely diffused Art Nouveau movement, interpreted differently in different countries: Jugendstil in Germany; Sezessionstil in Austria where it appeared in the disciplined designs of Otto Wagner (1841–1918), Josef Hoffmann (1870–1956) and the Wiener Werkstätte. Very much of its time, Art Nouveau was the last breath of the old world before the advent, in the early 20th century, of modernism, a movement which has encompassed all countries.

Though early American furniture may have been based on English styles and cabinetmaking it soon developed a simpler, more elegant style of its own (left).

Federal furniture – the American version of the Empire and Regency styles in Europe – shows the same linear designs, with an added element of comfort (below).

American

When England's American colonies were first founded, the colonists' own furniture naturally went with them and for many years furniture was either exported from the homeland or made in similar style by joiners and turners, who decorated pieces with linenfold or floral carvings. Needs were simple: in the parlour, a table and often a bed. Elsewhere, usually in the hall, were chairs, tables, chests and a settle.

By the end of the 17th century pieces of furniture were being made by cabinetmakers, sometimes English-trained. More functional than their English prototypes, pieces like chests and the new, all-purpose chests of drawers were popular, as well as dropleaf, stretcher and trestle tables. Around the same time, the newly arrived German and Swiss Mennonite settlers made furniture that was sturdier than English pieces and decorated with bright, painted motifs.

Colour was used in early American furniture to add an element of decoration to the simple shapes (above). This 18th-century painted chest is home to a collection of plovers and early wooden decoys (above right).

These ladder-back rocking chairs with their woven rush seats are based on the utilitarian simplicity of Shaker design (below). They are based on British country furniture, but are slimmer and taller.

designed furniture with function, on which no superfluous decoration was permitted. They made cupboards, chests and ladder-back chairs in maple, pine and fruitwoods.

During the 19th century, American furniture became heavier and more ornate, and at the end of the century there was, as in Europe, a reaction against the ostentatious. Simpler styles emerged, including an equivalent of Arts and Crafts, the furniture of Gustav Stickley (1857–1942) who made simple, almost rough-hewn furniture.

The twisted shapes of the furniture known as Adirondack is reminiscent of the English 19th-century craze for Chinese root furniture, which was made from knotty tree roots (left).

Gustav Stickley popularized the European Arts and Crafts Movement in America with his pieces of simple, sturdy furniture (below right).

A revolutionary designer, Charles Eames (1907–1978) used, in addition to more traditional materials, moulded plywood, metal and fibreglass (below).

By the 18th century, American furniture, while still retaining its functional aspects, had become far more sophisticated in appearance. Still based on English prototypes and the English pattern books that had been sent westwards (but more loosely), various obviously American styles made in cities like Boston, Philadelphia, New York and Charleston began to evolve, complete with local decorative details and adapted lines.

As the 18th century and the confidence of the American people progressed in tandem, they found that the relatively austere lines of neoclassical design appealed to the republican-minded hearts of this new nation. And thus exponents like Duncan Phyfe (1768–1854) in New York and Samuel McIntire (1757–1811) in Salem developed their own restrained form of neoclassicism – the Federal style – which veered towards but did not replicate the elegant lines of either the Regency or the Empire.

Other movements had a direct influence on contemporary and future furniture design. In the late 18th and early 19th centuries, a style of furniture was evolved by a religious sect known as the Shakers. Seeking union in all things, they

Eastern

From the earliest times, wooden furniture has been made in the Far East – particularly in China, Japan and India. Indeed, by the middle of the 3rd century, Chinese furniture was already well developed and included various designs for platforms, tables and stools. Chinese craftsmanship was subtle, and combined with a sure

understanding of form. The finest Chinese furniture was made between the 14th and 17th centuries, often from hardwoods like rosewood. Indian furniture, too, had been made for many centuries – at first in simple shapes, and later when Dutch, Portuguese and English colonists arrived, in more elaborate designs that more closely approximated to European forms.

By the end of the 16th century in the West, both the furniture and decoration of the mysterious East were much admired and imitated – particularly features like the woven-rattan bark caning that Indian furniture makers used for the backs and seats of many of their chairs. Bamboo furniture also became popular. Made both in China and India as early as the 2nd and 3rd centuries, furniture made from the hollow woody stems of various tropical grasses was designed to be expendable and was intended mainly for outdoor use. Specialist techniques of

An exotic chair made from horns and upholstered in an appropriate fabric design is next to a typically Eastern table of pierced wood and inlay (above).

The elegant lines of this antique Chinese table work well with the Western sofa it stands next to (above right).

An Indian castellated white-painted cupboard is given a new use as a filing cabinet of distinction (right).

hardwood ebony, which was chiefly used in the West for the making of extremely elaborate decorative cabinets, in conjunction with other exotic materials such as tortoiseshell and ivory. Black ebony was the most familiar form, though there were non-black forms such as Coromandel wood, which was grey-brown in colour, and which was named for its source on the eastern coast of India.

The striking lines of this Eastern X-frame table makes the ideal base for a detailed group of objects (far left).

Almost sculptural in its simplicity, this Eastern cupboard, with its dramatic butterfly lock, is emphasized by the simple vase (left).

A Chinese console table is all the more striking when set against a wall of plain colour with little other ornament (above).

A heavily carved, typically low Indian table looks as good outside at this East Hampton beach house as it would inside (below).

joinery were developed for its construction, bent pieces often being formed by growing the living plant material through a shaped sheath. Bamboo furniture soon became fashionable in the West. First original pieces were imported; later fake bamboo effects were achieved with paint techniques and carving.

And then there was, of course, the splendid art of lacquering. To begin with, examples of this decorative skill were imported from Eastern countries, but later European cabinetmakers were inspired to make their own – first cutting up pieces of imported lacquered screens and incorporating them into new pieces of furniture, later imitating Eastern lacquer with the new technique known as 'japanning', which involved the use of gesso, paints and varnishes.

The oriental woods, too, used for Eastern cabinetmaking were soon imported into the West – in particular, the exotic and very strong

credits

a = above t = top b = below l = left
r = right c = centre d = designed by

endpapers Piero Castellini Baldissera's house in Montalcino, Siena; **1** a house in East Hampton **d** Lars Bolander; **2–3 & inset 2l&r** John Rosselli's house in New Jersey; **2c** Lars Bolander's apartment in Palm Beach; **4** Annie Kuentzman-Levet's house in Bechères-sur-Verges; **4–5** Robert Kime's house in Wiltshire; **5** Michael & Ruth Burke's house in Mississippi **d** Vicente Wolf of Vicente Wolf Associates Inc.; **6** John Rosselli's house in New Jersey; **7l** John Rosselli's house in New Jersey; **7ar&c** Piero Castellini Baldissera's house in Montalcino, Siena; **7br** Annie Kuentzman-Levet's house in Bechères-sur-Verges; **8al** Christopher Hodsoll's house in London; **8bl&r** Sharone Einhorn & Honey Walters' shop Ruby Beets in Bridgehampton; **9al** John Rosselli's house in New Jersey; **9bl** Robert Kinnaman & Brian Ramaeker's house in Wainscott; **9r** Annie Kuentzman-Levet's house in Bechères-sur-Verges; **10–11** Frédéric Méchiche's house near Toulon; **12** a house in Paris **d** Yves Gastou, Galerie Yves Gastou; **13al** Philippa Rose's apartment in London **d** Caroline Paterson with furniture supplied by Leonie Lee of

Snap Dragon; **13cl** Bunny Williams' house in Connecticut; **13bl** Robert Kinnaman & Brian Ramaeker's house in Wainscott; **13br** Frank Faulkner's house in Hudson; **14** Frédéric Méchiche's apartment in Paris; **14–15** Frédéric Méchiche's apartment in Paris; **15** a house in Paris **d** Yves Gastou, Galerie Yves Gastou; **16** Julie Prisca's house in Normandy; **16–17** Sharone Einhorn & Honey Walters' shop Ruby Beets in Bridgehampton; **18l** Frédéric Méchiche's house near Toulon; **18ar** Wilson Kerr's London house; **18cr** Piero Castellini Baldissera's house in Montalcino, Siena; **18br** Julie Prisca's house in Normandy; **19** Frédéric Méchiche's apartment in Paris; **20al&c** Piero Castellini Baldissera's house in Montalcino, Siena; **20bl** John Rosselli's house in New Jersey; **20r** Michael & Ruth Burke's house in Mississippi **d** Vicente Wolf of Vicente Wolf Associates Inc.; **21al** Frank Faulkner's house in Hudson; **21ar&bl** Philippa Rose's apartment in London **d** Caroline Paterson with furniture supplied by Leonie Lee of Snap Dragon; **21br** Jason McCoy's apartment in New York; **22** a house in East Hampton **d** Lars Bolander; **23l** Michael & Ruth Burke's house in Mississippi **d** Vicente Wolf of Vicente Wolf Associates Inc.; **23r** a house in East Hampton **d** Lars Bolander; **24** John Rosselli's house in New Jersey; **24–25**

Robert Kinnaman & Brian Ramaeker's house in Wainscott; **25a** John Rosselli's house in New Jersey; **25b** a house in Paris **d** Yves Gastou, Galerie Yves Gastou; **26a** Frank Faulkner's loft apartment in New York; **26cl** a house in Pennsylvania **d** Laura Bohn of L.B.D.A.; **26c** a house in Paris **d** Yves Gastou, Galerie Yves Gastou; **26cr** Frank Faulkner's loft apartment in New York; **26b** a house in East Hampton **d** Lars Bolander; **27a** Bunny Williams' house in Connecticut; **27cl&c** a house in East Hampton **d** Lars Bolander; **27r** Galerie Yves Gastou; **27b** Philippa Rose's apartment in London **d** Caroline Paterson with furniture supplied by Leonie Lee of Snap Dragon; **28** Annie Kuentzman-Levet's house in Bechères-sur-Verges; **29al** Frank Faulkner's house in Hudson; **29ar** Frédéric Méchiche's house near Toulon; **29bl** a house in East Hampton **d** Lars Bolander; **29br** Frank Faulkner's loft apartment in New York; **30al** Michael & Ruth Burke's house in Mississippi **d** Vicente Wolf of Vicente Wolf Associates Inc.; **30ac** Christopher Gibbs's house in Oxfordshire; **30ar** Christopher Hodsoll's house in London; **30bl** Robert Kime's house in Wiltshire; **30br** Alidad's apartment in London; **31** Christopher Gibbs's house in Oxfordshire; **32al** Christopher Hodsoll's house in London; **32ar** Frank Faulkner's loft apartment in New York; **32br** Isabel Bird's house in London **d** Prue Lane; **32br** Piero Castellini Baldissera's house in Montalcino, Siena; **33l** a house in Paris **d** Yves Gastou, Galerie Yves Gastou; **33r** Frédéric Méchiche's homes in Paris & near Toulon; **34** Frank Faulkner's house in Hudson; **35al** a house in Paris **d** Yves Gastou, Galerie Yves Gastou; **35bl** Jason McCoy's apartment in New York, **35ar** Frédéric Méchiche's apartment in Paris; **35br** Jason McCoy's apartment in New York; **36ar** Annie Kuentzman-Levet's house in Bechères-sur-Verges; **36b** Philippa Rose's apartment in London **d** Caroline Paterson with furniture supplied by Leonie Lee of Snap Dragon; **36–37** Robert Kime's house in Wiltshire; **37a** L.D.V.'s house in Paris **d** Olivier Vidal; **37b** Frédéric Méchiche's house near Toulon; **38** Piero Castellini Baldissera's house in Montalcino, Siena; **39** Irene & Giorgio Silvagni's house in Provence; **40al** John Rosselli's house in New Jersey; **40ar** Wilson Kerr's London house; **40bl** L.D.V.'s

house in Paris **d** Olivier Vidal; **40br** Frank Faulkner's loft apartment in New York; **40–41** Sharone Einhorn & Honey Walters' shop Ruby Beets in Bridgehampton; **41a** a house in East Hampton **d** Lars Bolander; **41b** Christophe Gollut's apartment in London; **42–43** a house in East Hampton **d** Lars Bolander; **43** Christopher Gibbs's house in Oxfordshire; **44** Christophe Gollut's apartment in London; **44–45** Christopher Hodsoll's house in London; **45al** Philippa Rose's apartment in London **d** Caroline Peterson with furniture supplied by Leonie Lee of Snap Dragon; **45ar** Robert Kime's house in Wiltshire; **45b** Christopher Hodsoll's house in London; **46a** Christophe Gollut's apartment in London; **46c** a house in East Hampton **d** Lars Bolander; **46b** Alidad's apartment in London; **46–47** Irene & Giorgio Silvagni's house in Provence; **47a&bl** Alidad's apartment in London; **47c** Christopher Gibbs's house in Oxfordshire; **47br** a house in East Hampton **d** Lars Bolander; **48a** Frank Faulkner's house in Hudson; **48b** Frédéric Méchiche's house near Toulon; **49** Frank Faulkner's house in Hudson; **50l** a house in East Hampton **d** Lars Bolander; **51al** Alidad's apartment in London; **51bl** Lars Bolander's apartment in Palm Beach; **51br** Robert Kime's house in Wiltshire; **52** Christophe Gollut's apartment in London; **53al** Alidad's apartment in London; **53cl** Michael & Ruth Burke's house in Mississippi **d** Vicente Wolf of Vicente Wolf Associates Inc.; **53bl** John Rosselli's house in New Jersey; **53r** Alidad's apartment in London; **54–55** Lars Bolander's apartment in Palm Beach; **56a&bl** Frédéric Méchiche's house near Toulon; **56br** Robert Kime's house in Wiltshire; **57al** Robert Kime's house in Wiltshire; **57ar** Christopher Gibbs's house in Oxfordshire; **57bl** Irene & Giorgio Silvagni's house in Provence; **57br** Christopher Hodsoll's house in London; **58** Lars Bolander's apartment in Palm Beach; **59al** Lars Bolander's apartment in Palm Beach; **59cl** Christopher Hodsoll's house in London; **59bl** Frédéric Méchiche's apartment in Paris; **59ar** Annie Kuentzman-Levet's house in Bechères-sur-Verges; **59br** Galerie Yves Gastou; **60a** Frank Faulkner's loft apartment in New York; **60b** Piero Castellini Baldissera's house in Montalcino, Siena; **60–61** a house in East Hampton **d** Lars Bolander; **61cl** Frédéric Méchiche's

house near Toulon; **61bl** Michael & Ruth Burke's house in Mississippi **d** Vicente Wolf of Vicente Wolf Associates Inc.; **61r** a house in East Hampton **d** Lars Bolander; **62** a house in Paris **d** Yves Gastou, Galerie Yves Gastou; **62–63** Frédéric Méchiche's apartment in Paris; **63al** Galerie Yves Gastou; **63ar** Frédéric Méchiche's apartment in Paris; **63br** Robert Kime's house in Wiltshire; **64–65** John Rosselli's house in New Jersey; **66a** Robert Kinnaman & Brian Ramaeker's house in Wainscott; **66b** Annie Kuentzman-Levet's house in Bechères-sur-Verges; **66–67** Julie Prisca's house in Normandy; **68l** Christopher Hodsoll's house in London; **68ar** L.D.V.'s house in Paris **d** Olivier Vidal; **68br** Bunny Williams' house in Connecticut; **69l** Annie Kuentzman-Levet's house in Bechères-sur-Verges; **69ar** Robert Kinnaman & Brian Ramaeker's house in Wainscott; **69br** John Rosselli's house in New Jersey; **70** Piero Castellini Baldissera's house in Montalcino, Siena; **71l&ar** Piero Castellini Baldissera's house in Montalcino, Siena; **71br** Philippa Rose's apartment in London **d** Caroline Paterson with furniture supplied by Leonie Lee of Snap Dragon; **72a** Christopher Gibbs's garden in Oxfordshire; **72b** Bunny Williams' house in Connecticut; **73al** John Rosselli's house in New Jersey; **73ar&b** Christopher Gibbs's garden in Oxfordshire; **74a** John Rosselli's house in New Jersey; **74c** Bunny Williams' garden in Connecticut; **74b** Robert Kime's garden in Wiltshire; **74–75** Bunny Williams' garden in Connecticut; **75al,c&b** Bunny Williams' garden in Connecticut; **75ar** Christopher Gibbs's garden in Oxfordshire; **76** Christopher Gibbs's garden in Oxfordshire; **77l** Christopher Gibbs's garden in Oxfordshire; **77ar** John Rosselli's garden in New Jersey; **77br** Robert Kime's garden in Wiltshire; **78** Lars Bolander's apartment in Palm Beach; **78al** Lars Bolander's apartment in Palm Beach; **78bl** Christopher Gibbs's house in Oxfordshire; **79ar** Laura Bohn's house in Pennsylvania; **79br** Piero Castellini Baldissera's house in Montalcino, Siena; **80** Michael & Ruth Burke's house in Mississippi **d** Vicente Wolf of Vicente Wolf Associates Inc.; **80–81** Frank Faulkner's house in Hudson; **82al** Christopher Hodsoll's house in London; **82ar** L.D.V.'s house in Paris **d** Olivier Vidal; **82b** Frank Faulkner's house in Hudson; **82–83** Lars Bolander's apartment

in Palm Beach; **83a** Irene & Giorgio Silvagni's house in Provence; **83b** John Rosselli's house in New Jersey; **84a** Christopher Hodsoll's house in London; **84b** Annie Kuentzman-Levet's house in Bechères-sur-Verges; **84–85** a house in Paris **d** Yves Gastou, Galerie Yves Gastou; **85al** Julie Prisca's house in Normandy; **85ar** a house in East Hampton **d** Lars Bolander; **85bl** Frédéric Méchiche's house near Toulon; **85br** a house in East Hampton **d** Lars Bolander; **86–87** Frank Faulkner's loft apartment in New York; **88al** Wilson Kerr's London house; **88ar** a house in East Hampton **d** Lars Bolander; **88b** Frank Faulkner's loft apartment in New York; **88–89** Lars Bolander's apartment in Palm Beach; **90al** Robert Kime's house in Wiltshire; **90ar** a house in Paris **d** Yves Gastou, Galerie Yves Gastou; **90b** Lars Bolander's apartment in Palm Beach; **91al&b** Robert Kime's house in Wiltshire; **91arb** Robert Kime's house in Wiltshire; **92** Julie Prisca's house in Normandy; **93l** Julie Prisca's house in Normandy; **93ar** Irene & Giorgio Silvagni's house in Provence; **93cr** Robert Kime's house in Wiltshire; **93br** Frank Faulkner's loft apartment in New York; **94–95** Lars Bolander's apartment in Palm Beach; **96a** Frédéric Méchiche's house near Toulon; **96b** Irene & Giorgio Silvagni's house in Provence; **97a** Frédéric Méchiche's house near Toulon; **97b** Irene & Giorgio Silvagni's house in Provence; **98–99** Irene & Giorgio Silvagni's house in Provence; **99a** Philippa Rose's apartment **d** Caroline Paterson with furniture supplied by Leonie Lee of Snap Dragon; **99b** Wilson Kerr's London house; **100a** Piero Castellini Baldissera's house in Montalcino, Siena; **100bl** Irene & Giorgio Silvagni's house in Provence; **100br** Christopher Hodsoll's house in London; **101** Frank Faulkner's house in Hudson; **102a** Christopher Gibbs's house in Oxfordshire; **102b** Frédéric Méchiche's apartment in Paris; **103al** a house in East Hampton **d** Lars Bolander; **103ar** Irene & Giorgio Silvagni's house in Provence; **103b** Bunny William's house in Connecticut; **103br** Bunny William's house in Connecticut; **104a** Frédéric Méchiche's apartment in Paris; **104bl** Christopher Hodsoll's house in London; **104br** Frédéric Méchiche's house near Toulon; **105** a house in East Hampton **d** Lars Bolander; **106–107** Piero Castellini Baldissera's house

in Montalcino, Siena; **108–109** Frédéric Méchiche's apartment in Paris & house near Toulon; **110a** Christophe Gollut's apartment in London; **110b** Annie Kuentzman-Levet's house in Bechères-sur-Verges; **111** Alidad's apartment in London; **112** Lars Bolander's apartment in Palm Beach; **112–13** John Rosselli's summer house in New Jersey; **114a&ac** Robert Kime's house in Wiltshire; **114ar** Alidad's apartment in London; **114b** Isabel Bird's house in London **d** Prue Lane; **115al** Robert Kime's house in Wiltshire; **115ar** Frank Faulkner's loft apartment in New York; **116** a house in East Hampton **d** Lars Bolander; **117** a house in East Hampton **d** Lars Bolander; **118–19** L.D.V.'s house in Paris **d** Olivier Vidal; **120–21** Frank Faulkner's loft apartment in New York; **122a** Wilson Kerr's London house; **122b** Christophe Gollut's apartment in London; **123** Christophe Gollut's apartment in London; **124** a house in East Hampton **d** Lars Bolander; **125a** Frédéric Méchiche's house near Toulon; **125b** Frank Faulkner's house in Hudson; **126a** Michael & Ruth Burke's house in Mississippi **d** Vicente Wolf of Vicente Wolf Associates Inc.; **126bl** a house in Paris **d** Yves Gastou, Galerie Yves Gastou; **126cr** Robert Kinnaman & Brian Ramaeker's house in Wainscott; **126br** a house in Pennsylvania **d** Laura Bohn of L.B.D.A.; **127a** Isabel Bird's house in London **d** Prue Lane; **127b** L.D.V.'s house in Paris **d** Olivier Vidal; **128** Piero Castellini Baldissera's house in Montalcino, Siena; **128–29** Irene & Giorgio Silvagni's house in Provence; **129** Christopher Hodsoll's house in London; **130–31** Frédéric Méchiche's apartment in Paris; **131** a house in East Hampton **d** Lars Bolander; **132** a house in East Hampton **d** Lars Bolander; **132b** Michael & Ruth Burke's house in Mississippi **d** Vicente Wolf of Vicente Wolf Associates Inc.; **132–33** Michael & Ruth Burke's house in Mississippi **d** Vicente Wolf of Vicente Wolf Associates Inc.; **133a** Julie Prisca's house in Normandy; **133b** Christophe Gollut's apartment in London; **134l** Isabel Bird's house in London **d** Prue Lane; **134ar** Irene & Giorgio Silvagni's house in Provence; **134cr** Philippa Rose's apartment in London **d** Caroline Paterson with furniture supplied by Leonie Lee of Snap Dragon; **134br** Christopher Gibbs's house in Oxfordshire; **135al** Irene & Giorgio

Silvagni's house in Provence; **135bl** Frédéric Méchiche's apartment in Paris; **135r** John Rosselli's house in New Jersey; **136** Bunny Williams' house in Connecticut; **137al** Sharone Einhorn & Honey Walters' shop Ruby Beets in Bridgehampton; **137b** Julie Prisca's house in Normandy; **138a** Bunny Williams' house in Connecticut; **138bl** Frank Faulkner's house in Hudson; **138br** a house in Pennsylvania **d** Laura Bohn of L.B.D.A.; **139** Frédéric Méchiche's house near Toulon; **140–41** Frank Faulkner's house in Hudson; **141** Michael & Ruth Burke's house in Mississippi **d** Vicente Wolf of Vicente Wolf Associates Inc.; **142a** Robert Kime's house in Wiltshire; **142bl** Bunny Williams' house in Connecticut; **142br** a house in Pennsylvania **d** Laura Bohn of L.B.D.A.; **143a** John Rosselli's house in New Jersey; **143bl** Christopher Gibbs's house in Oxfordshire; **143br** Philippa Rose's apartment in London **d** Caroline Paterson with furniture supplied by Leonie Lee of Snap Dragon; **144** a house in East Hampton **d** Lars Bolander; **144–145** a house in East Hampton **d** Lars Bolander; **145** Frank Faulkner's house in Hudson; **146** Christophe Gollut's apartment in London; **147al** Piero Castellini Baldissera's house in Montalcino, Siena; **147bl&r** Christopher Hodsoll's house in London; **148** Frank Faulkner's loft apartment in New York; **148–149r** Sharone Einhorn & Honey Walters' shop Ruby Beets in Bridgehampton; **150** Irene & Giorgio Silvagni's house in Provence; **151a** Irene & Giorgio Silvagni's house in Provence; **151ba** house in East Hampton **d** Lars Bolander; **152** Frank Faulkner's loft apartment in New York; **152–53** Annie Kuentzman-Levet's house in Bechères-sur-Verges; **154** Irene & Giorgio Silvagni's

house in Provence; **154–55** Piero Castellini Baldissera's house in Montalcino, Siena; **156–57** Christopher Gibbs's house in Oxfordshire; **158** Michael & Ruth Burke's house in Mississippi **d** Vicente Wolf of Vicente Wolf Associates Inc.; **159la** house in East Hampton **d** Lars Bolander; **159ar** Philippa Rose's apartment in London **d** Caroline Paterson with furniture supplied by Leonie Lee of Snap Dragon; **159br** a house in Paris **d** Yves Gastou, Galerie Yves Gastou; **160a** Bunny Williams' house in Connecticut; **160l** Christopher Gibbs's house in Oxfordshire; **160br** John Rosselli's house in New Jersey; **161–63** Bunny Williams' house in Connecticut; **164** John Rosselli's house in New Jersey; **164–65** Robert Kime's house in Wiltshire; **165** Piero Castellini Baldissera's house in Montalcino, Siena; **166** Bunny Williams' house in Connecticut; **167a** Bunny Williams' house in Connecticut; **167bl** Lars Bolander's apartment in Palm Beach; **167br** Michael & Ruth Burke's house in Mississippi **d** Vicente Wolf of Vicente Wolf Associates Inc.; **168l** Annie Kuentzman-Levet's house in Bechères-sur-Verges; **168r** Christopher Gibbs's house in Oxfordshire; **169l** Bunny Williams' house in Connecticut; **169ar** Robert Kime's house in Wiltshire; **169br** Sharone Einhorn & Honey Walters' shop Ruby Beets in Bridgehampton; **170al** Piero Castellini Baldissera's house in Montalcino, Siena; **170ac** Bunny Williams' house in Connecticut; **170ar** Sharone Einhorn & Honey Walters' shop Ruby Beets in Bridgehampton; **170bl** Bunny Williams' house in Connecticut; **170br** a house in Pennsylvania **d** Laura Bohn of L.B.D.A.; **171** Sharone Einhorn & Honey Walters' shop Ruby Beets in Bridgehampton; **172–73** Frédéric Méchiche's apartment in

Paris; **176–77** Christopher Gibbs's house in Oxfordshire; **177** Robert Kime's house in Wiltshire; **178** L.D.V.'s house in Paris **d** Olivier Vidal; **179** Frédéric Méchiche's apartment in Paris; **180ar** Frédéric Méchiche's house near Toulon; **180cl** Irene & Giorgio Silvagni's house in Provence; **180br** Frédéric Méchiche's house near Toulon; **180–81** Wilson Kerr's London house; **181a** L.D.V.'s house in Paris **d** Olivier Vidal; **181b** a house in East Hampton **d** Lars Bolander; **182al** a house in Pennsylvania **d** Laura Bohn of L.B.D.A.; **182ar** Robert Kinnaman & Brian Ramaeker's house in Wainscott; **182b** Bunny Williams' house in Connecticut; **183a** Sharone Einhorn & Honey Walters' shop Ruby Beets in Bridgehampton; **183b** L.D.V.'s house in Paris **d** Olivier Vidal; **184al** a house in East Hampton **d** Lars Bolander; **184ar** Philippa Rose's apartment in London **d** Caroline Paterson with furniture supplied by Leonie Lee of Snap Dragon; **184b** Lars Bolander's apartment in Palm Beach; **185al** Michael & Ruth Burke's house in Mississippi **d** Vicente Wolf of Vicente Wolf Associates Inc.; **185ac&r** Philippa Rose's apartment in London **d** Caroline Paterson with furniture supplied by Leonie Lee of Snap Dragon; **185b** a house in East Hampton **d** Lars Bolander; **186** Bunny Williams' house in Connecticut; **187** Piero Castellini Baldissera's house in Montalcino, Siena; **188** Piero Castellini Baldissera's house in Montalcino, Siena; **192l** Christopher Hodsoll's house in London.

Architects and Designers

Alidad
Studio 4, The William Blake House
Bridge Lane
London SW11 3AD

Lars Bolander
240 Worth Avenue
Palm Beach, FL 33480
USA

Piero Castellini Baldissera
Studio Castellini
Via Morozzo della Rocco, 5
20123 Milan
Italy

Christopher Gibbs
3 Dove Walk
Pimlico Road
London SW1W 8PH

Christophe Gollut
116 Fulham Road
London SW3 6HU

Christopher Hodsoll Ltd
89–91 Pimlico Road
London SW1W 9PH

Wilson Kerr
15 Chepstow Place
London W2 4TT

Robert Kime
PO Box 454
Marlborough
Wiltshire SN8 3UR

Annie Kuentzman-Levet
2 Rue de Rouvres
28260 Bechères-sur-Verges
France

L.B.D.A.
Laura Bohn Design Associates
30 West 26th Street
New York, NY 10010
USA

Prue Lane
6 Formosa Street
London W9 1EE

Frédéric Méchiche
4 Rue de Thorigny
75003 Paris
France

Caroline Paterson
50 Lavender Gardens
London SW11 1DD

John Rosselli International
523 West 73rd Street
New York, NY 10021
USA

Olivier Vidal
10 Rue de Pentièvre
Paris
France

Bunny Williams Inc.
306 61st Street
Fifth Floor
New York, NY 10021-8752
USA

Vicente Wolf Associates, Inc.
333 West 39th Street
New York, NY 10018
USA

Shops and Galleries

Ruby Beets
1703 Montauk Highway
Bridgehampton, NY 11932
USA
American country antiques

Rupert Cavendish Antiques
610 King's Road
London SW6 2DX
United Kingdom
19th-century Biedermeier and Empire furniture

Galerie Yves Gastou
12 Rue Bonaparte
75006 Paris
France
Decorative arts of the 20th century

Robert Kinnaman and
Brian Ramaeker
2466 Montauk Highway
Bridgehampton, NY 11932
USA
Postal address:
PO Box 1140
Wainscott, NY 11975
American folk art and early painted furniture

Jason McCoy
41 East 57th Street
New York, NY 10022
USA
Fine arts

Julie Prisca Boutique
46 Rue du Bac
Paris
France
Lighting and accessories designed by Julie Prisca

Snap Dragon
247 Fulham Road
London SW3 6HY
United Kingdom
Eastern antiques and contemporary interpretations

index

Figures in italics refer to captions.

Acknowledgements

Some might say that it is far less work and much more play to visit America,
France and Italy, as well as England, simply to look at wonderful interiors owned
by some of the most inspirational, creative and inventive talents in interior
decoration — not to mention eating the delicious lunches that so many
owners pressed on us. Don't believe those cynics — it was of course
extremely hard work watching Fritz von der Schulenburg take his
wonderful photographs and, anyway, it was me who did the map
reading (from Tuscany to Palm Beach).

I also learnt much about the arrangement of rooms — that
subtle art of using objects and furniture in such as way that
combines harmony, beauty and comfort. It is an art that is
shared by all those whose houses and apartments we
photographed and talked to, and who were so
generous with their time and knowledge —
a little of which I have tried to pass on in this
book. I would like to thank
them all very much.

I was very lucky too that everyone at
Ryland Peters & Small was so
accommodating — and I would like
to thank in particular the saintly
Sian Parkhouse, as well as
Larraine Shamwana, Kate
Brunt, Nadine Bazar and
Maggie Town for their
patient, good-
tempered help.